That's Not in My American History Book

That's Not in My American History Book

A Compilation of Little-Known Events and Forgotten Heroes

Thomas Ayres

Taylor Trade Publishing
Dallas, Texas

Designed by Barbara Werden

Published by Taylor Publishing Company
1550 West Mockingbird Lane
Dallas, Texas 75235
www.taylorpub.com

Library of Congress Cataloging-in-Publication Data
Ayres, Thomas, 1936–
     That's not in my American history book : a compilation of little-known
  events and forgotten heroes / Thomas Ayres.
        p.   cm.
     Includes bibliographical references.
     ISBN 0-87833-185-9
        1. United States—History—Anecdotes. 2. United States—Biography—
  Anecdotes. 3. United States—History—Errors, inventions, etc. I. Title.

  E178.6 .A96 2000
  973—dc21   00-042603

10   9   8   7   6   5   4   3   2   1

Printed in the United States of America

To Isabel

Contents

Part Three

Scandals and Scoundrels
The Underside of History

Part Four

From Mutton Head to Slick Willie
Little-Known Facts about Famous People

⭐

That's
Not
in My
American
History
Book

viii

Part Five

The Vikings, Belle Starr, and Lucky Lindy

Myths That Became History

Acknowledgments

At a small country school nestled in a pine grove in the North Louisiana sand hills, a teacher named Mrs. Dees kept a disruptive eight-year-old after class one afternoon. Instead of having me dust erasers and clean the blackboard (punishments at which I had become adept with practice) she did something different that day. Ordering me to be seated, she opened a book and began to read to me. A half-hour later, she closed the covers and announced that I was free to go. I sat there, spellbound, lost in the story. I had to have that book and find out what happened to those people. The book was *Westward the Wagons*. It introduced me to a world of adventure filled with fascinating people from the past. From that day, I have not lost my fascination for the past and I have been a reader of books. Thank you, Mrs. Dees, for hooking me on reading.

While expressing gratitude, I must thank my literary agent, Jim Donovan, for his guidance and advice, as well as my old newspaper colleague and longtime friend, Bill Sloan, who encouraged me to send my manuscript to Donovan. To the editors at Taylor Publishing Company, especially Michael Emmerich and Fred Francis, I can only say thanks for your patience, and expert guidance, in bringing the seed of an idea to fruition.

Many contributed to the stories contained herein. Archaeology Professor Jon Gibson of the University of Louisiana at Lafayette, the foremost expert on native mound-building cultures in the lower Mississippi River Valley, has an ability to bring ancient cultures to life in a way even a layman such as myself can understand. Thanks are due the staff at the Russell Library at Middletown, Connecticut, for locating rare volumes detailing the flights of Gustave Whitehead; to Nina Johnson, at the Camp County Museum in Pittsburg, Texas; and Scott Thompson at the Louisiana State

That's
Not
in My
American
History
Book

x

Archives in Baton Rouge. There are others, far too numerous to mention. To all, I offer my gratitude.

Special thanks are due Travis Ayres, my brother and foot soldier, who helped with the research; Jerry and Benola Robinson and Sandy Bouy, who pried me away from my aging typewriter and introduced me to the wonders of Bill Gates's software; T. J. Hurst, for her help with the photographs and illustrations; and my wife Bea, who—with all due respect to Mr. Emmerich and Mr. Francis—is my ultimate editor in chief.

Finally, I want to thank those maverick historians who have stretched the boundaries of history by refusing to accept its myths—Richard Shenkman, Kenneth C. Davis, Irving and Amy Wallace, David Wallechinsky, J. P. Chaplin, James W. Loewen, Paul Kuttner, William O'Dwyer, Stella Randolph, and my old friend, Doug Storer, to mention only a few. You are my heroes.

THOMAS AYRES

Introduction

"Dad? Have you read about the Battle of Midway?"

"Sure."

"That was really something, huh? I mean how the whole course of the war was changed in only five minutes."

A warm feeling of pride swelled in my chest. I wanted to high-five the kid. My son, a college sophomore, had discovered World War II. His interest was not ignited in a classroom. The spark came from a video game. A desire to excel at the game had sent him to the library to research the battle. Fascinated, he began reading about other engagements and developed an interest in World War II aircraft. Finally, he got around to actually learning some of the reasons for the conflict.

It always disturbed me that my children did not share my enthusiasm for history. Occasionally, I would find one of their school texts lying around the house, thumb through its pages, and ask a question I considered common knowledge. Inevitably, I was shocked by their inability to answer and, worse still, by their seeming disinterest.

The sad truth is that today's students learn very little history. They shuffle through the pages with dull detachment because that is how most history texts are written. They sit through lectures on dates, events, and places as distant to them as the furthermost quasar, then guess at answers on multiple-choice tests. Is it any wonder we live in a time when a high school senior can pick up a diploma without knowing in which century the War of 1812 took place, much less the significance of Midway, Saratoga, Watergate, or Elizabeth Cady Stanton's suffrage convention?

History is not dates, places, and events to be memorized by school children. It is people influencing events—real people with blood coursing through their veins and thoughts through their

⭐

That's
Not
in My
American
History
Book

xii

minds. History breathes. Its heart beats. Just like those who make it, history changes and remains the same. It repeats its triumphs and tragedies. History is little people caught up in great events and great people turning insignificant events into momentous ones. History is madman and genius, warmonger, peacemaker, idealist, and cynic—actors all, playing out their roles on the greatest stage of all.

I am not a historian by training. Rather, I am a journalist who grew up in a time and place when television was in its infancy and children actually read books. For three formative years, I had the good fortune to attend a small country school where a portly woman named Mrs. Dees brought Washington, Jefferson, and Lincoln to life, stirred my imagination and sent me to the library to learn more. That school library consisted of one bookcase containing perhaps two or three hundred titles. But within those pages, I heard the creak of wagon wheels crossing the plains, the cries of Pickett's men as they stumbled into a storm of smoke and lead on Cemetery Ridge, and the drone of a small engine far out over the Atlantic as Lindbergh scanned the horizon for any sign of land.

Over the years, I developed an interest in historical trivia, those little stories around the edges of great events. I also discovered that many events recorded as history simply were not true. I learned that Betsy Ross was a fine seamstress but did not make the first American flag, and that she probably never met George Washington in spite of a picture right there in my history book showing them together. I learned that the Wright brothers were nice, industrious young men and their neighbors back in Dayton were proud of them, but they did not invent powered flight.

In the mid 1970s, I met a kindred spirit. His name was Doug Storer. If this book has a beginning, I suppose it begins with Doug.

He was small in stature and quite elderly when I met him but he seemed driven by a mysterious inner energy. His eyes would literally light with excitement when telling stories of his travels and adventures, which were far-ranging and many. For most of his life Storer was a researcher and writer for Robert Ripley's *Believe it or Not*. It was his job and passion to travel the world in a never-ending search for the unusual, the obscure, the unique, indeed, the unbelievable. He chronicled his encounters with strange people and bizarre events in *Believe it or Not* and later in his own *Amazing but True* books and newspaper columns.

For a brief time I was the young editor who reviewed the copy for his *Amazing but True* columns. Doug Storer was an editor's nightmare. He delighted in relating some bit of outrageous historical trivia that could not possibly be true, then, when challenged, he would smugly produce the source material. In retaliation, I found myself searching out obscure events and characters in an ongoing effort to stump him. Seldom was I able to do so.

It was Storer, his passion for obscure history, and his writings that inspired me to begin collecting the material found within these pages. The sources are varied—old newspaper clippings tossed into a file drawer over the years, magazine articles, little-known regional publications, obscure research papers, local and regional history books, and my own collection of history texts ranging from rare to current.

By no means is the material contained herein definitive history. It is anecdotal history, written more for entertainment than deep scholarly analysis. And, in spite of the title, much of the material *can* be found in history books—if you are willing to look hard enough. But these stories will not be found in the dull, traditional texts we expect our children to read. Here Benedict Arnold is the hero who saved the American Revolution before his own bitterness and a flirtatious teenage girl inspired him to betray it. Here the pathfinder of the American West is not John C. Fremont, but an African-American frontiersman who blazed the paths Fremont would follow. Here Albert C. Read is the first to cross the Atlantic in a fixed-wing aircraft, not Charles Lindbergh. Here pre-Columbian Native Americans were not savages, but intelligent people who built a great city and established a remarkable empire in the lower Mississippi River Valley 3,000 years before Columbus was born.

The reader's indulgence is requested in advance for the occasional opinionated observation that might weave its way into these pages. It results from an irrepressible genetic curse inherited from the maternal side of my family. I do not apologize for the occasional irreverent lance thrust at our hallowed institutions and sacred heroes. After all, irony and humor have never been missing from history—just from historians.

Concluding this introduction, I must say the collection of this material was a more enjoyable endeavor than the actual writing of the book. But if my son, the sophomore, is inspired to put aside his video game controller long enough to read it, I suppose it will have been worth the effort.

A Word about "Politically Correct" History

In recent years, there has been a trend in the academic community to place a priority on the inclusion of multiethnic history in our nation's story. Some call it multicultural history; others "politically correct" history. The supposition is that because our history was written by white males of European extraction, we are left with a narrow and somewhat distorted view of our past. The hypothesis is not without basis.

What about Native Americans, African-Americans, the Spanish, the Chinese, and others? Did they not contribute? Of course they did. Chinese and Irish sweat and muscle built the railroad that finally bound our nation together, and it was an African-American who discovered the pass through the Sierra Nevada Mountains that made it possible.

Without question, the inclusion of multiethnic history in our texts must be encouraged and applauded. For too long it was ignored. The danger, as is often the case, lies in extremism. When endeavoring to correct obvious distortions, we should never distort history just to be politically correct. It is already sufficiently distorted.

We cannot elude the fact that it was white male Europeans who set us upon the course that brought our nation and its people to this time in world history. Were they always right? Were they always just and good? Of course not. But what they left us is not all bad. Finally, we are a perking (sometimes boiling) melting pot of multiethnic peoples living under a system of laws borrowed from the French, English, Greeks, and Romans (and Iroquois, I might add) and still getting along reasonably well after two-and-a-quarter centuries of trial and error democracy. And although we are far from perfect and our system is far from perfect, it is an often-repeated truism that our revolutions still take place at the ballot box.

But what of the minority viewpoint?

There is an old Roman adage that says, "To the victor belong the spoils." A more recent American adage says, "Freedom of the press belongs to the man who owns the press." Both are applicable to the problem. If Germany had won World War II, European schoolchildren might be reading about the heroism of Nazi tank commanders in Belgium, no doubt ignoring the fact that their opponents rode horses and carried ceremonial spears.

The paths of American history are liberally sprinkled with such "ifs." If Native Americans had had sufficient numbers to initiate an eastward movement in the seventeenth century, there might not have been a westward movement in the nineteenth century. In that case we might be speaking an Algonquin dialect, be more ecologically correct, and live in small villages instead of large cities. That did not happen because three-quarters of the Native American population east of the Mississippi River was wiped out by smallpox epidemics in the sixteenth century. (Yes, they caught it from white male Europeans.) If France had had the foresight to transport its prison inmates to the upper eastern shores of North America instead of settling the St. Lawrence and lower Mississippi valleys, we might have a better appreciation for fine cuisine and fewer Taco Bells. If Spain had built a sufficient number of forts along the Sabine River and forbid Anglo immigration in Texas and California, we might be attending bullfights in Dallas and Beverly Hills.

These things did not happen.

The upper eastern shores of the United States were settled by Englishmen and Dutchmen. When they were not destroying native cultures, importing enslaved Africans, and feuding with each other and the king's governors, they managed to forge a mighty union of people of independent spirit and strength—enough strength to break the shackles of colonialism and form a nation that, in spite of its faults, remains the most respected on Earth.

The treatment of Native Americans as these white male Europeans muscled their way westward remains a genocidal disaster no matter who writes the history. Their maltreatment of enslaved African-Americans remains a horrible stain on our past and yet plagues our national psyche. These are things that did happen and they are a part of what our nation was and is.

Although we should not distort our history to be politically correct, we must expand it to include the minority viewpoint if we are to avoid an endless revisitation of the social plagues from our past. Only then can we hope to be better and do better than those who came before us.

PART ONE

Nolichunky Jack and Patriotic Horseflies

Stories Lost between the Pages

Did you know . . . ?
The Wright brothers were not the first to achieve powered flight? There was
a communist invasion in Texas eighty years before the Bolshevik revolution?
There was a fourteenth state, which the thirteen original ones would not let
join the Union? America's shortest war lasted only one day because the
opposing army got drunk? And could it be possible that the British legally
own California? If so, would this not be a good opportunity to give it back?
These are stories that, somehow, became lost between the pages of
history—some of them deservedly so. But others deserve a mention. For
example, did you know that a tribe of North American natives built a great
city, developed a knowledge of astronomy, and established trade routes that
extended thousands of miles 3,000 years before Columbus was born? They
even cooked their meals in "microwave" ovens. This is their story, along
with others that did not quite make the history books.

First in Flight
The Men Who Flew before the Wright Brothers

A small crowd of curious onlookers gathered at the edge of a field beside a windswept beach that August morning near the turn of the nineteenth century. They were attracted by the appearance of a strange machine and an even stranger man, who ignored them as he tinkered and made adjustments to the apparatus.

In answer to their questions, a newspaper reporter informed the onlookers that the contraption was a "flying machine." If they wanted to wait, they could watch the inventor attempt to make it fly—a prospect that drew expressions of doubt by some, and chuckles from others.

A murmur went through the crowd when the man finally climbed onto the craft and signaled to his young assistant to start the engine. As it sputtered to life, he revved the engine until it sounded right to him. Another signal, and the assistant and two volunteers towed the craft into position. Slowly, it moved forward on spindly wheels, gained speed, and then, to the astonishment of those who witnessed it, the winged wonder escaped the bounds of gravity. It rose steadily and traveled a remarkable distance before settling back to earth.

The setting was not Kitty Hawk, North Carolina, and the pilot was not Orville Wright. This event took place at Fairfield, Connecticut, on August 14, 1901, more than two years before the famous Wright brothers flight. The man on board the flying machine was a shy Bavarian immigrant named Gustave Whitehead.

For some a picture might be worth a thousand words, but for Gustave Whitehead, failure to have his aircraft photographed in flight was worth much more. It cost him a place in history.

Traditional history tells us the Wright brothers were the first to achieve "controlled" powered flight when their shaky aircraft lifted

★

That's
Not
in My
American
History
Book

4

itself from the beach at Kitty Hawk on December 17, 1903. It would be more accurate to state that they were the first to have a fixed-wing, motorized aircraft photographed in flight.

Manned flight in the United States had a colorful history long before the Wright brothers. In fact, the very first flight in America took place 110 years before the Kitty Hawk experience, and George Washington was there to witness it. A French aeronaut named Jean Pierre Blanchard demonstrated the then remarkable abilities of a hydrogen-filled balloon. During an exhibition for the president and dignitaries at Philadelphia, Blanchard and his balloon rose a mile into the air and traveled 15 miles in 46 minutes, finally coming to rest near Woodbury, New Jersey. Since Blanchard carried a message of introduction from President Washington on

Hang gliding, 1908 An unidentified volunteer soars on a glider designed by Gustave Whitehead.

First in flight Whitehead beat the Wright Brothers into the air by more than two years.

The airplane that beat the Wright Brothers

his flight, we might even stretch a point and call him the first airborne letter carrier in the United States.

A number of American inventors (not to mention those in England, France, and Germany) were experimenting with flight well before the Wrights. Two American engineers, Octave Chanute and A. M. Herring, were flying in experimental gliders on the shores of Lake Michigan long before the Wrights began exploring the possibilities of aviation. In 1896, Professor Samuel Pierpont Langley, Secretary of the Smithsonian Institution in Washington, D.C., constructed a small, fixed-wing airplane powered by a steam engine. He launched the unmanned craft from atop a houseboat on the Potomac River, and it traveled three-quarters of a mile at 20 miles per hour. However, the very first person to get a manned, motorized aircraft off the ground might have been an American inventor named Hiram S. Maxim. He constructed a multi-wing craft in England in 1894 and managed to get it into the air for a short hop.

In 1902, at Pittsburg, Texas, a preacher named Burrell Cannon was inspired to build an airship based on the description of the biblical flying machine in the Book of Ezekiel. Numerous witnesses watched a "Mister Stamps" fly the *Ezekiel Airship* almost two years before the Wright brothers' flight took place. Once in the air, the craft began to vibrate and the pilot had to shut off the engine and land it. The *Ezekiel Airship* was famous in its time. It was being transported to the St. Louis World's Fair for exhibit in 1904 when it was destroyed in a train accident. Cannon's airplane was rebuilt

**PART
ONE**
*Nolichunky
Jack and
Patriotic
Horseflies*

5

Whitehead (*holding his daugher*) sits beside Aircraft No. 22.

The Whitehead helicopter The inventor (*second from right*) stands beside his 1910 flying machine. The craft had 60 rotor blades—not enough to get it off the ground.

in Chicago in 1908, and a pilot named Wilder flew it. Unfortunately, Wilder flew it into a utility pole, destroying the craft and prompting Reverend Cannon to finally concede that, "God never willed that this airship should fly."

In fact, Texas was something of an aeronautical hotbed just after the turn of the century. There are reports that another inventor managed to get a motor-powered craft into the air near San Antonio. A less successful turn-of-the-century flight took place at Justin when an inventor tried to launch an aircraft from the roof of a two-story building. The duration of that flight was two floors.

And then there was Gustave Whitehead. While others, including the Wright brothers, were struggling to achieve "controlled flight," Whitehead accomplished it. Not only did he beat the

That's
Not
in My
American
History
Book

6

Wrights into the air, he set distance and altitude records that make the Kitty Hawk experience pale by comparison.

Unfortunately, Whitehead was an inventor and not a promoter. He had only a limited command of the English language and, at the height of his success, he was totally absorbed in his work to the exclusion of all else. Had he been aware of the value of publicity, he might be known today as the father of flight. Instead, he joined that large corps of unsung figures forgotten by history.

The Wright brothers knew the value of publicity. Although the exploits of others might be cloaked in doubt, there is no doubt the brothers flew an airplane at Kitty Hawk that chilly December day in 1903. Five witnesses were present. Even more important, Orville brought a camera. The witnesses were all young men who were waiting around the nearby Kill Devil Life Saving Station that morning. When they saw the Wrights making preparations to attempt a flight, they walked down to the site to watch. A single rail had been placed upon the sand to guide the aircraft in its takeoff attempt. Orville set up his camera and carefully focused it on the rail. He asked a young lifeguard named John Daniels to stand by and click the shutter if the flying machine rose above the rail.

Three days earlier, Wilbur had attempted to get the craft they had christened *The Flyer* off the ground and failed. Now it was Orville's turn. He lay flat on the lower wing, revved the engine, and loosed a restraining rope. The aircraft moved down the rail and rose, and Daniels snapped the shutter. The flying machine reached a height of 10 feet, wobbled, and fell back to earth after a flight of 120 feet. It had stayed in the air 12 seconds. The Wrights launched three more flights that day. On the fourth attempt, *The Flyer* traveled 852 feet and stayed in the air 59 seconds. Elated, the brothers sent the following telegram to their father back in Dayton, Ohio:

SUCCESS. FOUR FLIGHTS THURSDAY MORNING ALL AGAINST 21-MILE WINDS. STARTED FROM LEVEL WITH ENGINE POWER ALONE. AVERAGE SPEED THROUGH AIR 31 MILES. LONGEST 59 SECONDS. INFORM PRESS.

Daniels's dramatic photograph eventually appeared in newspapers and magazines around the world. It made its way into history texts and the Wrights became famous.

Poor Gustave. By the time the Wrights completed their flight, he already had flown a much more sophisticated machine to a height of 200 feet, traveled more than 7 miles, and executed a full turn.

Whitehead's Fairfield flight was not his first. Between 1897 and 1901, he completed several "hops" in a succession of aircraft he built while experimenting with various wing configurations and engines of his own design. Whitehead never considered these "hops" as actual flights. However, the flight at Fairfield was impressive enough to satisfy the demanding German that he, indeed, had flown an aircraft. Dozens of spectators witnessed the event. Years

PART
ONE
*Nolichunky
Jack and
Patriotic
Horseflies*

7

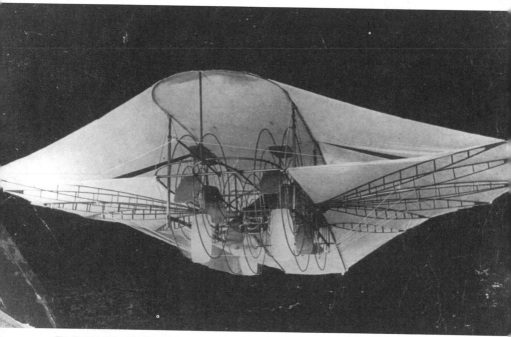

The Ezekiel Flying Machine A Texas preacher built this aircraft following a wheel-within-a-wheel concept described in the Bible. *Camp County Museum, Pittsburg, Texas*

later, many of them provided affidavits to back Whitehead's "first flight" claims. Among the witnesses that day was a newspaper reporter named Richard Howell. He wrote a full-page article about Whitehead and his flying machine in the August 19, 1901 issue of the *Bridgeport Sunday Herald.*

Whitehead's assistant, Junius Harworth, informed Howell that the airplane was "constructed entirely by Gustave Whitehead with

⭐

**That's
Not
in My
American
History
Book**

8

my assistance." Harworth described the craft, which he called No. 21, as a monoplane with a single engine that powered two propellers. Its body was constructed of spruce, pine, bamboo, and Japanese silk. In contrast to the Wright machine, which slid along a rail, Whitehead's aircraft taxied on bicycle wheels.

According to Howell, Whitehead's airplane took off in a field overlooking the beach near the end of Howard Avenue and landed near Wordin Avenue, a distance of about a half mile. He then turned the plane around and flew back, barely missing a small boy who ran in front of the craft as Whitehead was attempting to land it.

Gustave Whitehead was born Gustave A. Weisskopf in Leutershausen, Germany, on January 1, 1874. His early interest in aircraft is evidenced by the fact that he was building and flying gliders while still in his teens. He arrived in New York City in his early twenties and his first recorded appearance in America was in 1897 when the *New York Tribune* reported that a gasoline-powered airplane had been built by a Gus Whitehead at 139 Prince Street. The article noted that Mr. Whitehead was making plans to test his aircraft. A month after the article appeared, on November 24, 1897, Whitehead married Louise Tuba. On the marriage license, under occupation, he wrote "aeronaut."

The couple moved several times before settling in Bridgeport, Connecticut, in 1900. During that itinerant period, Whitehead made numerous short hops, witnessed by neighbors, friends, and fellow mechanics. His continuing effort to improve his aircraft finally resulted in the half-mile flight at Fairfield in 1901.

Whitehead would complete an even more impressive flight over Long Island Sound on January 17, 1902—still 23 months ahead of the Wrights. That aircraft, which he identified as No. 22, was constructed of steel and aluminum tubing, with 450 feet of silk covering the wings. Powered by a five-cylinder kerosene engine that drove twin propellers, it had a boat-like fuselage, making it amphibious. This time, Whitehead provided a personal account of the event in a letter (perhaps dictated, since he did not write English well) to *The American Inventor Magazine*:

> It was intended to fly only a short distance, but the machine behaved so well that at the first trial it covered nearly two miles over the waters of Long Island Sound and settled in the water without mishap.
>
> On the second trial . . . with myself on board, it sailed across

Long Island Sound. The machine kept on [course] steadily in crossing the wind at a height of about 200 feet when it came into my mind to try steering around in a circle. As soon as I turned the rudder and drove one propeller faster than the other, the machine turned round [sic] a bend and flew with the wind at a frightful speed but turned steadily around until I saw the starting place at a distance.

I continued to turn but when near the land again, I slowed up the propellers and sank gently on an even keel into the water. . . . She steadily floated like a boat. The length of the flight on the first was about two miles and on the second about seven miles. I consider the trip quite a success. . . . To my knowledge, it is the first of its kind.

PART
ONE
*Nolichunky
Jack and
Patriotic
Horseflies*

9

Two years later, the Wright brothers managed to get a much less sophisticated craft off the ground for a hop of 852 feet. But it was they and not Whitehead who reaped the glory and financial rewards that resulted from "man's first flight."

There were two reasons why Whitehead was denied his rightful place in aviation history. First, his accomplishments were overshadowed in a twenty-year publicity struggle between the Wright brothers and others for the fame and financial rewards that came with first-flight honors. Orville Wright and officials at the Smithsonian Institution both published articles dismissing Whitehead's flights as a hoax, despite numerous witnesses, including journalists and scientists. The second factor was prejudice. In the years leading up to World War I, a bitter propaganda campaign effectively demonized all Germans, including America's immigrants.

For a dozen years after the Wright brothers' flight, there was a blizzard of bizarre claims of aviation feats. Whitehead's achievement simply became lost in the publicity shuffle. The Smithsonian Institution would not acknowledge the Wright brothers' first-flight claim for more than twenty years, much less consider one accomplished by a German immigrant. When Daniels's Kitty Hawk photograph made its way into school textbooks, institute officials had little choice but to recognize the Wrights. Still, it was 1948 before the Wright family allowed *The Flyer* to be displayed at the Smithsonian. The family refused to donate the craft until Smithsonian officials signed a contract, agreeing to bestow the title "Fathers of Flight" upon the brothers.

Whitehead continued to refine his aircrafts and experiment with them for several years after his Long Island flights. While the

That's
Not
in My
American
History
Book

Wrights were secretive, Whitehead shared his designs and inventions. To raise money, he even sold his engines to other aviation pioneers. He did not bother to patent his aircraft until 1905. Even then, his ideas were widely copied by aircraft builders who ignored his patents.

In 1910 Whitehead took on the task of building a helicopter. The project attracted several investors but was doomed to failure. Instead of building a helicopter with a single rotor blade, Whitehead constructed one with no less than sixty propellers. Attempts to make it fly were unsuccessful. At age forty, broke, discouraged, and discredited, he took a job as a machinist in a Bridgeport manufacturing plant. He died in 1927 at age fifty-three.

For thirty-seven years, not even a gravestone marked Whitehead's resting place in the cemetery at Bridgeport; there was only a small bronze marker with the number 42 on it. It was 1964 when several members of the local Air Force Reserve Squadron became aware of the Whitehead story. They solicited donations and erected a proper headstone, finally paying tribute to the forgotten "aeronaut" who flew before the Wright brothers.

Nolichunky Jack and the Fourteenth State

Every schoolchild knows there were thirteen original states. But time and history have forgotten our fourteenth state—the one the others would not accept into the Union.

Our fourteenth state (actually, its founders called it an independent republic) existed for only four years, from 1784 to 1788. During that time it was a subject of continuous controversy and bitter debate. At one point, its governor came close to signing a treaty with Spain that would have been disastrous for the fledgling United States. He also almost got into a war with North Carolina. But what could one expect from a state that would elect a governor named "Nolichunky Jack?"

The fourteenth state covered an area of 29 million acres and was named after one of the nation's most illustrious founding fathers—Benjamin Franklin. It was called the Free Republic of Franklin.

The Franklin saga began in the early 1780s, when North Carolina's western border extended all the way to the Mississippi River. At the conclusion of the War for Independence, public funds were in short supply, and especially so in North Carolina. With the end of the war, hundreds of Carolinians crossed the mountains to settle in North Carolina's western wilderness. By 1784, the frontier inhabitants were demanding that North Carolina's government protect them from hostile Indians and roving bands of outlaws that plagued their settlements.

Most North Carolinians considered the western settlers to be little more than ruffians and outlaws themselves and did not want to spend their tax money to protect them. That prompted North Carolina Governor Alexander Martin to come up with a plan that proved politically popular with his constituents. He dumped the problem into the lap of the Continental Congress. At the urging of the governor, the North Carolina Assembly ceded its western lands

That's
Not
in My
American
History
Book

back to the Continental Congress, making that body responsible for protecting the wilderness region. What Governor Martin did not plan on was the fierce independence of the western settlers or the stubborn nature of Nolichunky Jack.

Jack's real name was John Sevier. A native Virginian descended from a French Huguenot family, his exploits as a frontier character were legendary. He was a hero at the Battle of King's Mountain during the War for Independence and before that had earned a reputation as a pathfinder and Indian fighter.

Shortly after North Carolina ceded the territory to the Continental Congress, Sevier and a group of his frontier cronies held a secession convention. On August 23, 1784, they declared North Carolina's western counties of Sullivan, Greene, and Washington to be independent. Sevier and his friends then held a constitutional convention and formed a provisional government they called the Republic of Franklin. Sevier was elected its governor.

The secession of the western counties did not concern Governor Martin. That was a problem for the Continental Congress. But the formation of an independent republic on his western border upset him mightily. He quickly moved to have the North Carolina Assembly reclaim the territory, but by then the Franklinites were enjoying their new status as a free state. North Carolina, they insisted, had no jurisdiction over their republic. Governor Martin responded by declaring the western territory in a state of rebellion and threatened to send troops to reclaim it. Sevier responded by vowing to raise an army to defend his republic.

On May 16, 1785, William Cooke, representing Franklin, arrived in New York to present to the Continental Congress a petition seeking statehood. Caught by surprise, North Carolina's delegation protested. Following a heated debate, a vote was taken. Seven states voted to admit Franklin to the Union. Although a majority, it fell two votes short of the required two-thirds needed for approval.

What followed was a period of chaos in Franklin. Because it had no means to back a currency, barter became the prevailing system of exchange. Governor Sevier's salary was fixed at 1,000 deer hides per year.

North Carolina would not give up its claim to the territory. In 1786, the North Carolina Assembly passed the Act of Oblivion. It promised to waive all back taxes if the citizens of Franklin would simply return to the fold. But, behind the scene, others were wooing Franklin. Across the ocean, Spain's monarchy was formulating a plan to form a number of frontier colonies into a Spanish alliance in North America. A minister from Spain arrived in Franklin, seeking Governor Sevier's cooperation. Had Sevier accepted the Spanish proposal, he might have become a wealthy man; but he turned it down.

Ignoring Franklin's claim of independence, North Carolina sent its own officials into the republic, creating two sets of authorities and a great deal of confusion. Rival clerks of court issued mar-

PART
ONE
*Nolichunky
Jack and
Patriotic
Horseflies*

**The infamous
Nolichunky Jack**
John Sevier led the charge to found the independent Republic of Franklin. .
Tennessee Conservation Department

riage licenses and recorded land transactions. Rival justices handed down conflicting decisions, and rival sheriffs got into fistfights. It seemed everyone was in control—and no one. Taxes went unpaid because no one was sure to whom they should be paid.

In exasperation, William Cooke wrote to Benjamin Franklin, urging him to intervene on behalf of the republic that bore his name, pointing out that the region was in a state bordering on anarchy. As it turned out, the aging Franklin was so far out of touch he was not even aware the troubled republic was named for him. In a letter of reply dated August 12, 1786, he noted: "I had never

That's
Not
in My
American
History
Book

14

before been acquainted that the name of your new state had any relation with my name, having understood that it was called Frankland."

Franklin went on to suggest that representatives from Franklin and North Carolina approach Congress to serve as a mediator. But North Carolina's legislative delegation was working behind the congressional scenes. In November of 1787 Congress decided that a new state could be admitted to the Union only after affirmation of nine of the thirteen states "and the consent of the state that originally claimed the territory." North Carolina had won the legal battle, but the ever-combative Nolichunky Jack was not about to give up.

In desperation, Governor Sevier turned once more to Spain, requesting a defense loan to protect Franklin's citizens from a military invasion by North Carolina. However, before a deal could be struck, a company of North Carolina law officers, led by John Tipton, invaded Franklin to arrest Sevier, clap him in irons, and spirit him back across the mountains. He had barely settled in his jail cell when a contingent of frontiersmen from Franklin showed up to break him out of jail and escort him back home.

By then, Sevier had realized the futility of continuing the struggle. In February of 1788, he and other leaders of the ill-fated venture crossed the mountains into North Carolina and surrendered to authorities. They stood trial, but their only punishment was to take an oath of allegiance to the State of North Carolina.

Ironically, Sevier would become a state senator representing Greene County in the North Carolina legislature. Also odd: As soon as things settled down, North Carolina once more ceded the same territory back to the federal government. This time it was accepted by Congress, and the "Territory of the United States of America South of the Ohio River" was formed. On June 1, 1796, a new state was created from the territory that once had been the troublesome Republic of Franklin.

They named it Tennessee. Its first governor was none other than the illustrious Nolichunky Jack Sevier.

The Great Communist Invasion of Texas

 Seventy years before czarist Russia fell to the Bolsheviks and plunged the world into three-quarters of a century of ideological conflict, there was another concerted effort to establish a utopian birthplace for communism—in Texas!

Frontier Texas attracted men for many reasons. They arrived seeking adventure, cheap land, elbow room, and independence. Some, like Davy Crockett and Jim Bowie, came looking for a fight; others were running away from one. Among those who fled there seeking freedom from political persecution were hundreds of European communists. They came with dreams of establishing the perfect society.

The great communist invasion of Texas lasted less than ten years, from 1847 to 1856. It had an unlikely beginning in the 1830s in the drawing rooms of Europe's intellectual elite, where French philosopher Charles Fourier's theories on communal socialism were being discussed and debated. Fourier envisioned a utopia organized in small, economic units called phalanxes, each containing 1,620 persons. His concept for a perfect society soon spread to university campuses and evolved into a movement that actually threatened existing governments. There were riots in the streets in France and Germany, and the governments of both countries responded with a brutal suppression of the movement.

Secret societies formed, and believers gathered to discuss alternatives to the current situation. Perhaps in America they could find the freedom to practice socialism. And in America was a place called Texas, an unspoiled land of fertile plains, clear streams, game in abundance, and forests heavy with fruit. They knew this was true, because that is how Prince Solms-Braunfels described it in his writings and lectures.

Prince Solms-Braunfels had visited Texas in 1844 and upon his return to Germany became a promotional guru for the region. He lectured at the universities of Giessen and Heidelberg and wrote

**That's
Not
in My
American
History
Book**

glowing, sometimes fictional, accounts of his adventures there. When writing about Texas, his pen dripped milk and honey.

Spellbound by his stories were members of a club named "Adelsverior," whose members called themselves "The Men of the Forties." It became their goal to establish a communal colony in Texas. By 1847 they had collected enough funds to attempt such a venture.

A tract of land was purchased through an agent and an advance party of thirty-three young men, most of them students, was selected to make the voyage. They were to construct buildings, plant a crop, and prepare for the thousands who would follow them.

In July of 1847, the party landed at the Port of Indianola on the Texas Gulf Coast. In his journal, a member of the group named Reinhardt described their inland trip:

> Twenty-four ox wagons had been waiting for us three weeks since Meuseback, the general agent of the Adelsverein, had seen to everything. We had supplies of every kind imaginable. For instance, complete machinery for a mill, a number of barrels of whiskey and a great many dogs, of whom Morro was the largest. We came prepared to conquer the world.

Describing an overland journey that required four weeks, he wrote: "We camped on the prairie and sang, drank and enjoyed ourselves as only the German student knows how to do. We lived like gods of Olympus and our favorite song on this tour was, *A Free Life We Lead.*"

In what is now Llano County in south Texas, the party stopped beneath a great live oak tree beside the picturesque Llano River.

"Here we camped, putting our wagons in a circle," Reinhardt wrote. "We constructed a big tent in the center, planted our cannon and put out a guard. Feeling perfectly secure in our fortified camp, we celebrated that night until three o'clock in the morning . . . We gave 'lebe hoch United States, lebe hoch Texas' for we were all good patriots."

They built an arbor-type, open-sided building 22 by 40 feet with a fireplace that measured 12 feet across. Then they began constructing houses. They named the village Bettina, after Bettina von Arnim, a noted authoress of the day. The Germans became friendly with Chief Satanta and his dreaded Comanche warriors.

A treaty was signed, to which both Comanches and settlers remained faithful. On one occasion, when supplies were stolen from the Germans, Satanta himself pursued the thieves and returned the goods. When the settlers' cattle strayed, the Comanches returned them.

By the summer of 1848, the men of Bettina no longer sang their songs, for there was little to celebrate. They had arrived too late to plant an adequate crop the previous summer, and a drought had wiped out the one that spring. During that time, Reinhardt learned a lesson that would take the Soviet leaders of the next century seven decades to discover:

> Since everyone was to work only if he pleased and when he pleased, the result was less and less work done as time progressed. Most of the professional men wanted to do the directing and ordering while the mechanics and laborers were to carry out their plans. Of course, the latter failed to see the justice of the ruling so no one did anything.

Bettina was abandoned the following fall. Several members of the group tried to establish a small commune named Darmstaedter Farm near what is now the town of New Braunfels. After two years, they sold the farm for one-fourth of its original cost.

Even as the dream of Bettina was crumbling, a new venture was beginning just north of San Antonio. In a beautiful valley where Sister Creek joins the Guadalupe River, a group of German scholars and gentlemen farmers established a community that became known as Sisterdale. One inhabitant described the cultural climate of the settlement as follows:

> A library of the ancient and modern classics was to be found in almost every home and the latest products of literature were eagerly read and discussed at the weekly meetings of these gentlemen farmers at the schoolhouse. . . . It sometimes occurred at these meetings that Comanches stood listening at the open door while one of the farmers was lecturing on the socialistic theories of St. Simon or Fourier.

Sisterdale survived as a semi-socialistic community far longer than the others, perhaps because its residents were more inclined to discuss socialism than practice it.

⭐

PART
ONE
*Nolichunky
Jack and
Patriotic
Horseflies*

17

That's
Not
in My
American
History
Book

18

By the late 1840s, several attempts had been made to establish communal colonies in Texas. The French communist followers of Etienne Cabet came to Texas with grand plans. It was their intention to establish "Icaria"—described as "A Republic of Unity and Brotherhood." The Republic of Icaria was to contain ten self-sustaining communes (or states) controlled by a central government.

Under the guidance of a Doctor Connough, 150 French immigrants landed at Galveston in 1849 and trudged 300 miles to the wilds of north Texas. Their goal was to establish a settlement on the banks of Denton Creek, 30 miles north of Dallas, near the present-day town of Justin.

Promoters who sold them the land promised that cabins would be waiting, but upon their arrival the immigrants found not a single structure. The Icarians hurriedly constructed flimsy shelters in preparation for cold weather. They were ill prepared for the brutal winter of 1849, and with the howling winds came a mysterious fever. By spring, more than half of the settlers were dead. Most of the survivors packed up and went north to join a French settlement in southern Illinois. Others took refuge in Dallas.

The final attempt to establish a large-scale commune in Texas took place just west of Dallas in the mid 1850s. Called La Reunion, it was to be the ultimate utopia. The venture was dreamed up by French, Swiss, and Belgian intellectuals who followed the Fourier school of social reform. One of the movement's most dedicated followers was a former French army officer named Victor Considerant, who resigned his commission to lead the first group of settlers.

Considerant planned to purchase 57,000 acres of land in west Texas for the settlement. Another 50 acres were to be purchased near Houston to serve as a point of disembarkation for the colonists who, he was certain, would flock to La Reunion by the thousands. It was the intention of the promoters to divide La Reunion into phalanxes—small, self-sufficient communities numbering 1,600 residents. Each phalanx was to occupy a league of land. The state was to advance money to get each phalanx started, but the funds had to be repaid. That was the plan. The reality was much different. Everything that could go wrong with the La Reunion dream did so.

Before he had a chance to purchase any land, Considerant learned to his dismay that, because of a misunderstanding, some two hundred colonists had set sail from Antwerp and would be arriving at Galveston at any time. Forced to act immediately, he purchased 2,000 acres of land three miles west of Dallas at a then exorbitant price of $7 per acre. The transaction consumed much of his cash, preventing him from acquiring the 57,000 acres in west Texas.

**PART
ONE**
*Nolichunky
Jack and
Patriotic
Horseflies*

19

In April of 1855 more than two hundred weary, footsore Europeans trudged into Dallas, having walked the 275 miles from Galveston. From the beginning, Considerant urged the organizers in Europe to send him settlers who were carpenters and farmers. Those who arrived were artists, watchmakers, professors, musicians, writers, and dance masters. Their inability to cope with frontier life was immediately evident. Their very first chore was to brand a newly purchased herd of cattle. It required an entire day to brand just twenty-five head, and they so botched the job that several men from Dallas had to be called in to complete the task.

The crops the colonists planted that summer produced only modest yields, and the houses they constructed were inadequate to cope with one of the most severe winters in Texas history. Having survived the winter, they planted their crops the following spring, unaware they were about to become the victims of a most unusual act of nature. In May of 1856, the Trinity River froze over as a blizzard howled across Texas. For days, the residents of La Reunion shivered helplessly in their homes. When spring finally returned, it brought a drought, followed by a plague of grasshoppers. The only crop that survived was wheat, not a marketable crop in 1856 Dallas.

One of the first to leave La Reunion in disgust was Considerant himself, but there was never a mass exodus. La Reunion simply melted away. By 1860, less than fifty people remained in the village; and in 1865, the courts ordered the public sale and liquidation of the property. Among the assets auctioned off was a large portrait of Fourier.

Although communal socialism was a dismal failure in Texas, the men and women who came seeking their utopia eventually contributed to the culture and commerce of Texas and the nation. Allyre Bureau of La Reunion became a famous orchestra leader and wrote the music that later was adopted for "The Trolley Song," made popular when Judy Garland sang it in the movie, *Meet Me in St. Louis.* Julien Reverchon became a famous naturalist. From Bettina, Gustave Schleicher became a famous Texas Ranger and later a U.S. representative. Dr. Ferdinand von Herff introduced the use of chloroform in surgery to the Southwest. Admiral Chester A. Nimitz, commander of U.S. forces in the Pacific during

That's
Not
in My
American
History
Book

World War II, descended from the German immigrants of south Texas. La Reunion professionals and businessmen helped Dallas become a cultural and commercial hub.

Of all the original ventures, only Sisterdale survived as an identifiable community. However, the descendants of all the German, Dutch, French, Swedish, and Belgian settlers are still found throughout Texas. German influence especially is evident in the architecture and culture of south Texas towns like New Braunfels, Schieicher, Schulenburg, Bergheim, and Luckenbach.

Meanwhile, deep in the scenic south Texas hill country, at a crossroads southwest of Sisterdale, sits a little farm town. Its name is Utopia, Texas.

National Horsefly Day

Stop the band! Hold the speeches! Take down those banners and snuff out the fireworks! Independence Day is not the Fourth of July. It should be the Second of July.

No one seems to know how it happened, but for well over 200 years we have been celebrating our independence from Great Britain on the wrong day. American independence was declared on July 2, not July 4. Little of great importance took place on July 4, 1776 at Independence Hall in Philadelphia, except for approval of the wording of the Declaration of Independence by the Continental Congress. In fact, the most significant event of that day might have been initiated not by the congress, but by a horde of giant horseflies that invaded Independence Hall.

Although British soldiers and local militias had been shooting at each other for more than a year, there was only guarded talk of outright independence from Great Britain when the congress met that fateful summer in 1776. Most colonial leaders still wanted equality with Englishmen, not separation from them. Many in congress still sought a compromise solution.

It was June 7, 1776 when Richard Henry Lee of Virginia stood before the Continental Congress and called for a clean break with England. He insisted it was time for the colonies to become "free and independent states." Many of those present were sympathetic to those sentiments, but few were willing to take such drastic action. To vote yes would be an act of treason, punishable by death. So the assembly did what politicians traditionally do when faced with a tough decision: They tabled Lee's motion for additional study.

When the congress met again on July 2, there had been a marked change in attitude. Recent actions by the British had inflamed passions. Lee's motion for a declaration of independence was brought back before the assembly and this time passed without a single dissenting vote. That night, John Adams penned the following sentiments in a letter to his wife, Abigail, back in Boston:

> The Second day of July, 1776, will be the most memorable in the history of America. I am apt to believe it will be celebrated by succeeding generations as the Great Anniversary Celebration.

On July 4, the Continental Congress met for only one item of business. Thomas Jefferson had written an official Declaration of Independence, and the delegates were there to debate its contents and approve the final wording. Jefferson's Declaration had been widely discussed prior to the meeting, and it seemed everyone had something to add or delete. As the session got underway, both the rhetoric and the temperature began to heat up inside Independence Hall. One congressman wanted to change the phrasing of a particular sentence. Another wanted to eliminate a direct reference to the King of England.

It was humid in Philadelphia that day, and as the delegates debated and mopped their brows, the windows of Independence Hall were opened to catch any breeze that might stir. Instead of a breeze, through the windows came an invasion of giant horseflies from a nearby stable. As the hungry horseflies descended on the founding fathers, debate ceased. A tormented delegate rose to suggest that Jefferson's declaration seemed suitable to him. Others in the assembly agreed. A motion of approval was made and quickly passed. The delegates just as quickly exited the building, swatting at horseflies.

Contrary to common belief, the Declaration of Independence was not even signed on July 4. The signing took place on August 18, 1776. Some members who could not attend on that date signed later. The final signature was not placed on the document until January 18, 1777. In the final analysis of the events of that summer, it can only be concluded that independence was declared on July 2 and the wording of the Declaration of Independence approved on July 4.

Although we managed to get the date wrong, July 4, 1776 remains an important day in American history, and every citizen should be grateful to the lowly horsefly for making it so. Had it not been for the intervention of horseflies at Independence Hall, Jefferson's Declaration of Independence, universally recognized as one of the greatest documents ever written, might have been scrambled into semiliterate, political gibberish.

Perhaps it would be more appropriate to celebrate July 2 as Independence Day and reserve the Fourth of July to honor the horsefly for its contribution to preserving our nation's most cherished document.

Horsefly invasion At Independence Hall, a horde of horseflies ended debate over the final wording of the Declaration of Independence. *National Archives & Records Administration*

Do the British Own California?

At a time of growing resentment over foreign ownership of United States assets, it might be upsetting to Californians to learn that not only does their state belong to Great Britain, but its real name is New Albion.

On June 17, 1579, Sir Francis Drake claimed the area now known as California in the name of the Queen of England. By right of discovery and with the consent of the natives who occupied the region, he planted a flag and posted a declaration of claim. To this day, Drake's claim has not been challenged, and Great Britain has never ceded the territory to the United States.

For many years, historians were aware that Drake probably had reached the coast of California during his sixteenth-century circumnavigation of the world. In 1936, evidence was found to confirm it.

On the north shore of San Francisco Bay, near the Golden Gate Bridge, a shop clerk named Beryle Shinn picked up a rock and saw what looked like a piece of brass buried in the soil. He unearthed a rather large, dirt-caked metal plate and took it home. He placed it in his garage and forgot about it. Eight months later, while curiously examining the piece of metal, he noticed what appeared to be writing and attempted to clean it with soap and water. He could make out the word "Drake," but could not decipher the remaining symbols.

Shinn took the plate to Dr. Herbert Bolton at the University of California, where it was thoroughly cleaned and its message was revealed:

BEE IT KNOWNE VNTO
ALL MEN BY THESE PRESENTS
IVNE 17, 1579
BY THE GRACE OF GOD AND IN THE NAME OF

**PART
ONE**

*Nolichunky
Jack and
Patriotic
Horseflies*

Discoverer of California
Sir Francis Drake claimed
for England the territory
now known as California.
*Dictionary of American
Portraits*

HERR MAIESTY
QVEEN ELIZAVETH OF ENGLAND AND HERR
SVCESSORS FOREVER
I TAKE POSSESSION OF THIS KINGDOM
WHOSE KING AND
PEOPLE FREELY RESIGN THEIR RIGHT AND
TITLE IN THE WHOLE
LAND VNTO HERR MAIESTIES KEEPING NOW
NAMED BY ME AND
TO BEE KNOWNE VNTO ALL MEN AS
NOVA ALBION.
FRANCIS DRAKE

    Dr. Bolton presented his find to the California Historical Society and set off an international debate on the authenticity of the plate. It has passed every scientific and historical test.

    Drake's sixteenth-century voyage is documented in detail in his logs and journals. After plundering New World Spanish settlements, Drake had sailed around the tip of South America with Spanish warships in pursuit. In an effort to escape, Drake hopscotched the western coastline of Central and North America, searching for the fabled Northwest Passage. Sailors of that era

That's
Not
in My
American
History
Book

26

were convinced that somewhere there existed a water passage across the North American land mass connecting the Atlantic and Pacific oceans.

Drake apparently sailed into what is now San Francisco Bay looking for such a passage. In his journals he described how, on one of his stops, the native inhabitants thought they were being visited by gods and offered him gifts, including their lands. That, of course, was Drake's interpretation of the event. A more likely scenario might have had Drake asking the natives if they objected to his claiming their lands for England and, since they did not understand a word he was saying, he graciously accepted their silence as consent. Regardless of the circumstances, Drake evidently had a plaque erected to commemorate the claim. It was that plaque Beryle Shinn found 357 years later.

Fortunately, the British have not pursued their claim during the ensuing years. Perhaps it is because the Royal Family has experienced enough recent adversity without adding such further headaches as earthquakes, smog, horrific traffic jams, riots, wildfires, mud slides, and screenplay-wielding amateur screenwriters.

A Civil War Story
The Origin of "Taps"

More than a century has passed since the Civil War traumatized our nation and left scars that required many generations to heal. It was a war that divided not only the nation, but states, cities, villages, neighborhoods, and households. Some 680,000 Americans died in that conflict—more than in all other U.S. wars combined, from the Revolution through Desert Storm. That total does not even include the many civilian casualties. Some communities lost most their of adult male populations, because it was not unusual for a company from a particular locale to be effectively wiped out by a single volley or cannon bombardment.

From out of that horrific war came many stories of inspiration, but few to equal the saga of Capt. Robert Ellicombe of the Union Army. The Civil War frequently pitted kinsman against kinsman, but Ellicombe's story illustrates the ultimate tragedy of that circumstance.

During the Union's Peninsula Campaign in the summer of 1862, in the aftermath of a battle near Harrison's Landing, Captain Ellicombe and his men came upon the bodies of several dead Confederate soldiers. The captain ordered his men to prepare the bodies for burial. As graves were being dug, Ellicombe inspected the corpses and was horrified to discover that one of the bodies was that of his son.

The boy had been studying music at a school in the South when the war began. Communications between them had been cut off but Ellicombe was confident his son was safe since the boy was supposed to be far removed from the fighting. The captain was devastated to discover in so brutal a way that his son had left school and joined the Confederate Army.

When the boy's personal items were handed to Ellicombe,

That's
Not
in My
American
History
Book

28

Adapting "Taps"
Gen. Daniel Butterfield
presented his bugler with the
music to "Taps" after it was
found on a Confederate
casualty.
Dictionary of American Portraits

among them he found a folded scrap of paper. Carefully drawn on it were several bars of music.

Captain Ellicombe went to his commanding officer and asked if he might be permitted to bury his son with full military honors behind Union lines. When permission was granted, he sought out the company bugler and showed him the notes on the paper. Ellicombe asked him if it would be possible to play the notes at his son's service. It was a simple composition and the bugler assured him he could play it.

At the conclusion of the services for young Ellicombe, the low, haunting sounds of the melody from the bugle sent chills down the spines of those present as it drifted across the countryside.

The following day Division Commander, Gen. Daniel Butterfield, summoned his bugler, Oliver Morton, to his headquarters. He handed Morton a piece of paper and asked him to arrange the notes on it for a new bugle call. It is not known whether Butterfield heard the music at young Ellicombe's funeral and inquired about it, or if Captain Ellicombe simply gave it to him.

Morton arranged the new call and began playing it for Butterfield's troops. It was a beautiful melody, but so simple in its composition that other buglers easily picked it up and played it for their units. By the end of the war, the call was being played throughout the Union Army. It is called "Taps."

Today, "Taps" is the official "lights out" call for all of the U.S. military services. Its mournful melody marks the end of a soldier's day—and the end of his life. It is traditionally played at military funerals and on special holidays like Memorial Day, Veterans' Day, and the Fourth of July. And those few notes once penned by a schoolboy soldier have been adopted as the bugle call for the military forces of many nations and are now played around the world.

PART
ONE
Nolichunky
Jack and
Patriotic
Horseflies

29

The Insult That Nearly Sparked the Revolution

A nurse with a sharp tongue and an independent nature almost touched off the American Revolution prematurely. This little-known episode in American history took place at Salem, Massachusetts, on February 26, 1775, well before the revolution became a shooting war at Lexington and Concord. Principals in the incident were a fiery young woman named Sarah Tarrant and a British soldier with a low tolerance for insult.

On that fateful Sunday, war was the furthest thing from the minds of Salem's citizens. With temperatures hovering in the twenties, almost everyone was inside, huddled beside their hearths. But there was plenty of activity outside Boston, where British soldiers under the command of Col. Alexander Leslie were forming ranks. The colonel had information that the rebels were hiding a cannon at Salem, and he was determined to confiscate it.

The best description of what happened when the British arrived at Salem that day is contained in the writings of one William Gavett, who was only a boy when he witnessed the events. Gavett's journal not only gives an eyewitness description of what happened but also provides rare insight into the mind-set of colonial citizens and British soldiers at that tense time and place in history.

> My father came home from church rather sooner than usual, which attracted my notice and said to my mother, "The regu-lars are coming and they are marching as fast as they can. . . . I wish to keep the children home."

But young Gavett was not about to stay home and miss the excitement. He slipped out of the house and watched the redcoats approach the town.

"It was very cold that day and the soldiers were without overcoats and they shivered exceedingly," Gavett wrote. "Many of the inhabitants climbed onto the leaf of the drawbridge and black-guarded the troops . . . calling [the] soldiers red-jacketed lobster-coats and damnation to your government."

Village elders arrived to plead with the rebel youths sitting on the drawbridge to stop taunting the troops for fear there would be bloodshed. Colonel Leslie ordered the rebels to lower the bridge and allow his soldiers to cross it, but they refused. When the British considered using a nearby boat to cross the stream, Joseph Whicher went into action. According to Gavett's account:

> One Joseph Whicher, the foreman at Colonel Sprague's distill-ery, was at work scuttling the colonel's gondola and the soldiers ordered him to desist and threatened to stab him with their bay-onets if he did not . . . Whereupon, he opened his breast and dared them. They pricked his breast so as to draw blood.

The boat having been scuttled, the British commander once more ordered the rebels to lower the bridge.

"I will get over this bridge before I return to Boston if I stay here until next autumn," Gavett quoted the colonel.

James Barr, described by Gavett as "An Englishman and a man with much courage," began arguing with Colonel Leslie. "This is not the King's highway," Barr insisted. "It is a road built by the owners of the lots on the other side and no king, country or town has anything to do with it."

After several minutes of debate, Colonel Leslie, aware that armed militiamen were arriving on the scene, offered a compro-mise. If the rebels would lower the bridge, he would march his sol-diers fifty rods into the town and then return to Boston. By then it was obvious that the British officer wanted only to save face and get his men safely back to Boston without igniting hostilities. At the urging of the town elders, the young rebels finally lowered the bridge.

The colonel crossed the bridge at the head of his troops, went precisely fifty rods, turned his columns, and started back. There were hoots and taunts from the citizens as the redcoats made their way back toward the bridge.

In those volatile times, every town and village had a militia, in-cluding Salem. By the time the British began crossing the bridge, armed militiamen were taking up positions behind fences and houses. Word of the confrontation at the bridge also had spread to

That's
Not
in My
American
History
Book

nearby communities, and scores of armed men were en route to Salem.

It was then that Sarah Tarrant entered the drama. She had been watching from her window, which was so close to the street she could almost reach out and touch the passing soldiers. Finally, her patriotic zeal would not allow her to remain silent. She leaned from the window and shouted:

"Go home and tell your master he has sent you on a fool's errand. . . . Do you think we were born in the woods to be frightened of owls?"

Her insult proved too much for the pride of one British soldier. He promptly stepped from the ranks and aimed his musket directly at Sarah.

"Fire if you have the courage," she challenged him, "but I doubt if you have it."

Colonel Leslie ordered the soldier back into line, but he refused to budge. For several breathtaking seconds he stood there with musket aimed, even as Sarah continued to berate him. Finally the soldier lowered the weapon, turned, and ran back to his place in the ranks. The relieved colonel quickly led his troops out of town.

Had the soldier fired his weapon by accident or on purpose that day, the war would have erupted at that instant. It also is likely that the British contingent would have been badly mauled, because they were exposed to dozens of militia rifles aimed at them. Just two months later, hostilities would erupt at Lexington and Concord when "the shot heard 'round the world" was fired.

If that shot had been fired at Salem that cold February day, Sarah Tarrant would have gone down in history as the woman who started the American Revolution.

Away Down South in . . . Ohio?
Strange Origins of America's Music

If an Englishman wrote our national anthem, would it be asking too much to believe that a Yankee wrote "Dixie"? And if you believe that, could it be possible a Southerner wrote the music to "The Battle Hymn of the Republic" or that a vice president of the United States composed a song that became a number-one hit and stayed at the top of the recording pop charts for six weeks?

It's all true. Some of America's most cherished music came to us along some very circuitous, unlikely paths.

Almost everyone knows that Francis Scott Key wrote the words to "The Star-Spangled Banner." However, few are aware that an Englishman wrote the music. John Stafford Smith did not set out to write an anthem for the United States, a nation with which his native England would fight two wars in his lifetime. He originally composed the melody for a London social club in the late 1700s. He had no way of knowing it would become, in order, a religious hymn, a popular drinking song in the pubs of London and America and, finally, the anthem of the United States of America.

Likewise, Key could not know that the words of his patriotic poem would be sung to the tune of an English drinking song and become his nation's anthem 117 years after he wrote it.

The United States did not even have an official anthem until 1931. That is when Doug Storer, a researcher for *Ripley's Believe it or Not,* became aware that the United States had never adopted an anthem. "The Star-Spangled Banner" had been performed at sporting events for years and played as the U.S. anthem at the Olympic Games, but never officially designated as the nation's anthem.

Informed of this, songwriters from New York to Hollywood composed patriotic songs and urged their congressmen to submit them for consideration. It was debated that "The Star-Spangled Banner" was not appropriate, because it was difficult to sing and people could not remember the words.

★

That's
Not
in My
American
History
Book

34

But, at the urging of Storer and others, the U.S. Congress created an act in 1931 officially naming "The Star-Spangled Banner" the anthem of the United States. Regretfully, Francis Scott Key and John Stafford Smith were not around to collect royalties.

If an Englishman wrote the national anthem, is it possible to convince a Southerner that a Yankee wrote "Dixie"? Or would a Yankee believe a Southerner wrote the inspirational music to "John Brown's Body" and "The Battle Hymn of the Republic"?

"Dixie," the song that has endured for more than a century as the anthem of the South, was written in 1860 by a New York song-and-dance man named Dan D. Hammett. Whatever his inspiration, it was not those old cotton fields back home, and Hammett definitely was not born on a frosty morn down in Dixieland. He was born in Ohio and penned "Dixie" while sitting in his New York hotel room.

Hammett performed the song on stage in New York, and it was a popular tune in the months prior to the outbreak of the Civil War. With the beginning of hostilities, Confederate soldiers adopted the song as their own. Ironically, the song also was one of Abraham Lincoln's favorite tunes.

As for the music for "The Battle Hymn of the Republic," it originally was composed as a religious hymn by a Southern songwriter named William Steffe. It became the favorite marching song of Union soldiers, who sang the words of "John Brown's Body" to its lively cadence.

The inspirational words of "The Battle Hymn of the Republic" were written by Julia Ward Howe, a staunch abolitionist, suffragist, and poet. She was married to Samuel Gridley Howe, a leading abolitionist, and while visiting Washington, D.C., with her husband in the summer of 1861, she went with friends to a parade ground to watch a grand review of Gen. George McClellan's troops. The soldiers were marching to the music of William Steffe's hymn, and Mrs. Howe was inspired by the music and the pageantry of it all. She later wrote that, as she returned to her room at the Willard Hotel, the music continued to play in her mind. She awoke in the middle of the night, still hearing the tune.

"As I lay there waiting for the dawn, the long lines of the desired poem began to twine themselves in my mind," she would write. She got out of bed and, struggling with a broken pen, began putting the lines on paper.

PART
ONE
*Nolichunky
Jack and
Patriotic
Horseflies*

35

Mine eyes have seen the glory of the coming of the Lord,
He is trampling out the vintage where the grapes of wrath are stored. . . .

She sold her poem to *Atlantic Monthly Magazine* for four dollars. It was published in February of 1862. Within months, "The Battle Hymn of the Republic" was on the lips of almost every Northern soldier. It remains a popular hymn to this day.

Many other American classics also had surprising beginnings.

The old drinking song, "How Dry I Am," originally was a hymn written by two preachers before tavern patrons decided to change the words and keep the melody. George Gershwin once wrote a song about the "Pee Dee River." His brother thought he could do better and looked through an atlas until he came across the Suwannee River in Florida. He convinced Gershwin to change the lyrics to "Swanee River."

"Home Sweet Home" was perhaps the nation's most popular song of the last half of the nineteenth century. It was a favorite song of the men on both sides in the Civil War, and regimental bands traditionally ended their evening camp concerts with its haunting melody. It was not unusual for the bands of opposing armies to join together and play "Home Sweet Home" even as the encamped soldiers of North and South solemnly waited for the battle that would come with dawn. Ironically, John Howard Payne, the man who wrote the lyrics, was a traveling actor who lived in

Top of the pops
Vice President Charles G. Dawes composed a tune later adapted and made a 1958 No. 1 hit.
Chicago Historical Society

★

That's

Not

in My

American

History

Book

36

hotel rooms and boarding houses his entire life, and never had a home.

A similar story is that of Albert von Tilzer, who wrote "Take Me Out to the Ball Game" and performed it on vaudeville stages. Von Tilzer never saw a baseball game until twenty years after he wrote the song.

So who was the vice president who wrote a number-one pop hit?

It was Charles G. Dawes, who served under President Calvin Coolidge from 1925 to 1929. Dawes wrote the music, originally titled "Melody in A Major," in 1912. Tommy Edwards recorded it in 1958 for MGM Records under the title "It's All in the Game." The song quickly climbed to No. 1 on the pop charts, stayed there for six weeks, and eventually sold more than a million copies.

Unfortunately, like John Stafford Smith and Francis Scott Key, Dawes was not around to collect royalties for his work.

The Original Cleveland Indian

Today he is long forgotten, his name and deeds obscured by the passing of the seasons. But for many years, when old-time baseball players got together and the subject came around to the greatest who ever played the game, someone was sure to bring up the name of "Sock" Sockalexis.

Louis "Sock" Sockalexis never won a batting title. He never led the major leagues in home runs or hits or runs batted in. In fact, he never completed a full season in the major leagues. Yet, for decades after his tragic death, many who saw him perform would passionately argue that he was the best who ever played the game. And they would insist that, had he not been plagued by misfortune, he would have surpassed the records of all of baseball's greats.

Almost everyone is familiar with the story of Jim Thorpe, whose football, track, and baseball exploits are legend. Sockalexis is the Native American super-athlete who preceded Thorpe. A member of the Penobscot nation, he was born on a reservation across the river from Old Town, Maine, in 1871. He came from the influential Bear Clan, of which his grandfather was chief.

Sockalexis was still a teenager when his amazing athletic ability was spotted by a visiting priest, who befriended the youth and introduced him to the baseball coach at the Catholic school in Van Buren, Maine. The coach encouraged the boy to enroll, and from his first day on the field it became apparent that Sockalexis was born to play baseball. He moved with unusual speed and grace, making plays that others would not even attempt. His smooth swing with the bat sent line drives beyond the outfielders. Almost immediately, he captured the attention of college coaches.

In 1893, Sockalexis enrolled at Holy Cross College in Worcester, Massachusetts, and batted .444 over two seasons. At the urging of the Notre Dame baseball coach, he transferred there in 1895. But he did not complete a full season at Notre Dame. A scout for

That's
Not
in My
American
History
Book

the major league Cleveland Spiders saw him play and signed him to a contract.

The young man arrived in Cleveland behind a circus-like barrage of publicity extolling his talents. The ball club's promoters saw in Sockalexis a vehicle to fill the home stands. He was a hero before he even put on a uniform. Among the stories that circulated was one that he once threw a baseball 600 feet across the Penobscot River from his reservation to Old Town on the other shore. However, one phase of the publicity especially disturbed him. The newspapers shortened his name to "Sock" to better fit into limited headline space. When players and fans began calling him "Sock," it upset him because he was very proud of his name.

The sportswriters ballyhooed the occasion of his debut, for it marked the first time a Native American had played in a major league baseball game. The stands were packed for the occasion. The Cleveland fans expected great things from "Sock"—perhaps too much. Yet, in his first game, he only added to the growing legend.

Facing "Sock" on the mound was Amos Rusie, the famous New York Giants curveball artist. Rusie had been outspoken in a newspaper interview before the game, flatly stating that he was going to "strike out the Indian." Instead, "Sock" promptly slapped one of Rusie's famous curveballs over the fence for a home run, setting off a wild celebration.

Sockalexis batted .338 in only sixty-six games that season, a remarkable performance for a rookie who had joined a major league team in mid season. But that was not good enough for the Cleveland fans. They wanted him to hit a home run every time he came to the plate and often expressed their displeasure when he failed to do so. On the road, Sockalexis had to contend with scornful war whoops chorusing from the stands. He became a daily target for critical stories written by cynical sportswriters.

In addition to his unwanted celebrity, Louis Sockalexis discovered something else that summer in the big leagues. He found that whiskey could help him cope with racial harassment. Almost overnight, he became an alcoholic. He never played a second season.

How good was Louis Sockalexis?

Hugh Jennings, who managed the Detroit Tigers from 1907 to 1921, said he was the best he had ever seen. Jennings wrote of him:

He should have been the greatest player of all times—greater than Cobb, Honus Wagner, Nap Lajoie, Rogers Hornsby and any other of the men who made history for the game.

★

PART
ONE
*Nolichunky
Jack and
Patriotic
Horseflies*

Unable to adjust to a cynical world he could not understand and unable to return in disgrace to his own people, Sockalexis isolated himself and tragically drank himself to death. He was buried at Old Town, across the road from the Penobscot Indian Baptist Church and just down the road from the ball field where it all began.

Many years later, in 1934, a newspaper editor who remembered the legend of the great Indian ball player came upon the grave by accident. He was shocked to find the final resting place of Louis Sockalexis marked only by a rotting wooden cross. He wrote a series of articles soliciting contributions for a proper stone and bronze marker. The plaque, adorned by two crossed bats beneath a baseball, reads simply:

*In memory of Louis Sockalexis, whose athletic
achievements while at Holy Cross and later with
the Cleveland major league baseball team won
for him national fame.*

But the story does not end there.

When Sockalexis was playing for Cleveland, sportswriters for rival teams dubbed the team "The Indians." The name soon replaced Spiders and, more than a century later, the team remains the Cleveland Indians.

The shortest war ever fought by the United States lasted only one day and took place against an independent state located within the United States. It happened in 1867 against a self-styled republic named the Free State of Van Zandt.

Before declaring itself a free state and getting into a war, Van Zandt was just another county in sparsely populated east Texas. Because of its isolation, Van Zandt County and its inhabitants were generally ignored by occupying federal troops following the Civil War. But many of the residents resented the very idea that they were under the rule of a Yankee military officer.

That is why, in the summer of 1867, a large number of citizens gathered at the old brick courthouse on the town square in the town of Canton. Before the day was over, delegates from various communities had been elected. The delegates in turn called a convention, at which they voted to secede from the State of Texas and the United States of America.

Following procedures used by the founding fathers at Philadelphia, the delegates produced a Declaration of Independence, which concluded with the proclamation that "Van Zandt, henceforth, will be a free and independent state and will be known as the Free State of Van Zandt."

When word reached Gen. Philip Henry Sheridan in New Orleans that a new nation had been formed in the territory under his command, he immediately ordered a cavalry unit dispatched to Van Zandt to put down the rebellion. When word reached Canton that U.S. troops were on the way, Van Zandt's founding fathers called an emergency meeting. They had not anticipated that the U.S. Army would react in such a forceful way over a simple secession from the Union, apparently having forgotten that the nation had just completed a four-year war over that very issue. As the meeting progressed, the speeches became more fiery and concern turned to anger. The delegates finally reached a decision. They declared war on the United States.

Van Zandt citizens, armed with rifles and shotguns, gathered at the Canton town square, determined to defend their homeland against the impending invasion. History does not record the commander of that ragtag military organization, or even if it had one. But they marched to the national border (the county line) and took up defensive positions in the dense forest flanking the main road to Canton.

For the U.S. soldiers approaching Van Zandt that morning, the mission was regarded as little more than a casual ride in the country. The last thing they expected was an armed ambush; but as they came around a bend in the road, sporadic gunfire erupted from the underbrush some distance away.

Although well out of range of the guns, the cavalrymen were nevertheless startled. Seeing confusion in the ranks, the officers quickly ordered a retreat. To the Van Zandters, still firing their weapons, the retreat looked like a rout as the soldiers jerked their mounts about and galloped back down the road.

As gunsmoke drifted into the treetops, the Van Zandt defenders sent up a victory cheer. They had won the battle, and the blue coats would think twice before trying that again. The Van Zandt volunteers joked and swapped stories all the way back to Canton, where they converged on the tavern to celebrate their victory. The celebration lasted longer than the battle, continuing through the afternoon and well into the evening.

Meanwhile, once the U.S. officers had settled their troops, they resumed their march on Canton. Under cover of darkness, they cautiously crossed the border and rode, unopposed, all the way into town. What they found was a party on its last legs. Those Van Zandt defenders who had not been dragged home by irate wives and mothers were promptly rounded up and shackled. Canton, the free-state bastion of independence, fell without a shot being fired.

The following morning, the Van Zandt patriots awakened with splitting headaches and Yankee guards standing over them. The federal officers, however, also had a problem: They had almost a hundred rebels under guard with no means to house or feed them and absolutely no idea what they should do with them. A rider was dispatched to summon a circuit judge and to wire for orders from superiors. Meanwhile, the commander sent some of his men to fell

That's
Not
in My
American
History
Book

42

trees with which they constructed a crude prison stockade. But fate, the elements, and William Allen were about to intervene on the side of the Van Zandt prisoners.

Allen, an ex-Confederate soldier who had spent the final year of the Civil War in a Union prison camp, was prepared for just such an event. Instinctively, he had hidden a knife in his boot before going off to battle that morning. He spent two nights sawing on a weak link in the chain that ran through the ankle shackles securing the prisoners. On their second night of confinement, a downpour drenched the men in the stockade and sent the guards seeking shelter. The chain was removed from the shackles. The rain had loosened the poles of the stockade, and several were removed from the back of the structure. To the last man, the rebels escaped into the night.

Once free, they scattered to seek out friendly farmers to free them from their ankle shackles. Most of the Van Zandters fled across the Sabine River to the dense swamplands of western Louisiana. Another group, William Allen among them, headed for the Oklahoma Territory. After hiding out in Oklahoma for several months, Allen made his way to Arkansas, where he went to work for a doctor and began studying medicine.

Not one of the free state rebels ever went to trial. Although arrest warrants were issued, none were served—and there is no evidence that the Army wasted much time looking for the escapees.

Several years after the event, Dr. William Allen returned to Van Zandt County with his wife and children. The wounds of Reconstruction had healed. The soldiers had gone back north to their homes and families, and the arrest warrants lay forgotten somewhere in a musty file drawer.

Dr. Allen became a prominent member of the community and lived out a fruitful life in Van Zandt County caring for the sick and infirm.

The rebellion? Although history might have forgotten it, others did not. A sign on a highway leading into Canton, Texas, today reads simply:

YOU ARE ENTERING THE FREE STATE OF VAN ZANDT.

Saga of the *American Turtle*

If asked when the submarine made its first appearance in combat, most Americans would answer World War I. But the first submarine was launched during the American Revolution, 137 years before World War I began. Unfortunately, its debut turned out to be more comical than auspicious.

The first submarine was christened the *American Turtle*, and the name was appropriate. It was the brainchild of a bookish, 31-year-old Yale University student named David Bushnell.

As tensions increased between the American colonists and King George III in the early 1770s, the students at Yale passionately debated the consequences of war versus peace. The strongest argument against war with England was the might of the British Navy. Opponents of armed revolt pointed out that, should the colonies go to war, all King George had to do was blockade the eastern seaboard. Such an action would doom any insurrection.

While his fellow students were theorizing, Bushnell hatched a plan to combat a British blockade by blowing up ships anchored outside American ports. If he could build a craft that could sneak, unseen, beneath the water, the operator might be able to attach explosives to the hulls of enemy ships. One man would be capable of sinking an entire fleet.

Bushnell began his project by conducting a series of tests to determine if gunpowder would explode underwater. He was gratified to discover that, with the proper fuse, it could be done.

When fighting finally broke out between the colonists and British soldiers in 1775, Bushnell left Yale to devote himself full time to building his underwater war machine. Returning to his hometown of Saybrook, he began building a strange contraption. His workshop was a remote shed beside the Connecticut River, well away from the prying eyes of some of his loyalist neighbors.

Upon completion, his craft did not look like an instrument of

★

That's

Not

in My

American

History

Book

44

destruction. In fact, Bushnell's submarine resembled a giant, tar-coated egg. It had fin-like paddles protruding from the sides and two pipes jutting from one end. The craft featured two foot-controlled pumps, enabling the pilot to surface and submerge at will. It also had a 700-pound keel and rudder.

Bushnell's submarine was built to accommodate one man. He calculated that the operator could close the hatch and paddle along at about three miles per hour beneath the surface of the water. Designed into the *American Turtle* were portholes, a compass, and a glass tube that would tell the operator where he was going and the depth of the craft. Once beneath a British ship, the operator would use an auger to bore a hole in the hull and attach a charge of 150 pounds of dynamite. A gunlock flint was adapted to set off a fuse, allowing the submarine to get away before the explosion took place.

Having completed his submarine, Bushnell approached colonial military leaders and informed them of his invention. Although skeptical, they arranged for him to transport his *American Turtle* to Long Island Sound. By then a full-fledged war was under way, and it was decided the vessel would be tested under actual combat conditions. Instead of piloting the craft himself, Bushnell somehow convinced his brother to take the controls.

For several days, Bushnell's brother practiced operating the craft in the waters of Long Island Sound, until he became expert at maneuvering it beneath the water's surface. Finally, a date was set for the *American Turtle* to blow up a British warship. Its target was the HMS *Eagle*, anchored in the river channel. However, as the time approached for Bushnell's brother to embark on his mission, he announced that he was not feeling well and, in fact, was much too ill to undertake such an operation.

On hand to observe the mission was a young soldier named Ezra Lee. After some convincing, he agreed to pilot the craft and made a couple of test runs to acquaint himself with the vessel. On the night of September 7, 1776, a decision was made to attack the *Eagle*.

Under cover of darkness, a whaleboat towed the *American Turtle* into the channel and as close to the *Eagle* as it could go without being detected. Still it required most of the night for Lee to orient himself and maneuver his vessel into position. Dawn was beginning to break when he finally brought the submarine near the hull of the *Eagle*. In his report of the events, Lee would write:

★

**PART
ONE**
*Nolichunky
Jack and
Patriotic
Horseflies*

45

I could see the men on deck and hear them talking. I then shut down all doors, sunk down and came up under the bottom of the ship . . . I came up with the screw against the bottom but found it could not enter. I pulled along to try another place but deviated a little to one side and immediately rose with great velocity and came above the surface then sank again, like a porpoise.

Lee tried to guide the submarine against the hull for another attempt, but by then it was daylight, and he decided to retreat before being detected. Although he was not seen by crewmen on the ship, Lee had no way of knowing that he had been spotted by British soldiers on shore. Baffled by what appeared to be the back of a giant turtle protruding out of the water, an officer assembled several riflemen. They piled into a rowboat and set out to check on the strange object bobbing beside the *Eagle*.

The soldiers were within fifty yards of the *American Turtle* before Lee spotted them. Knowing that he could not outrun the rowboat, he made a patriotic decision. Rather than allow the submarine to be captured, he would blow it up with himself and the soldiers in the rowboat. He lit the fuse to the magazine and headed the submarine straight for the boat. The sight of such a strange craft bearing down on them was too much for the soldiers. They began rowing, frantically, toward the shore.

"They returned to their island to my infinite joy," he would write. Having lit the fuse to the explosives, Lee had no choice but to release the magazine and try to distance himself from it. "I then weathered [sic] the island and our people, seeing me, came off with a whaleboat and towed me in. The magazine, after getting a little past the island, went off with a tremendous explosion, throwing up large bodies of water to an immense height."

The attack was a failure. Bushnell later concluded that the *Eagle* must have had a metal underplate that prevented the auger from penetrating the hull. Without a hole in the hull, there was no way to attach explosives to the ship.

Although the *American Turtle* was a failure as an instrument of destruction, Bushnell's concept for an underwater fighting machine would survive.

During the Civil War, Confederate engineers built several submarines, but only one saw action—the *H. L. Hunley*. On February 17, 1864, the *Hunley* rammed a torpedo into the Union warship USS *Housatonic*, sinking it in the harbor at Charleston, South

That's
Not
in My
American
History
Book

Carolina. The *Hunley* and its crew went down with the victim. It was the first time a submarine sank a ship.

By 1945, in the wake of two world wars, submarines had sent hundreds of ships to the bottom of the world's oceans. Bushnell's folly had become one of the most deadly instruments of war ever devised by man.

Old Civilizations of the "New World"

 On October 12, 1492, the natives on a small island in the central Bahamas discovered Christopher Columbus. They found him lost on their beach, along with several equally pallid companions who could not speak well enough to be understood and all of whom obviously had an atrocious sense of fashion. If the natives had been able to understand the gibberish spoken by these strangers, they would have been surprised to learn that, although he did know where he was, Columbus was claiming their island for Spain—wherever that was.

In fact, Columbus did not discover America on October 12, 1492, and contrary to the traditional first chapter of most school textbooks, American history does not begin on that date. In fact, Columbus did not even discover the Central Bahamas. The Tiano natives who migrated there from South America beat him to it by 800 years.

North America had a history long before Columbus's voyages opened European floodgates to the Western Hemisphere. Nomadic clans had come together to form crude cultures that evolved and splintered. Wild plants had been nurtured to produce food. Creek-bank settlements had become villages, and then villages cities, and from the cities grew great empires that prospered and disappeared. By the time Europeans arrived, more than 600 distinct cultures had evolved in the Americas. Far from being ignorant savages, the inhabitants were merchants and farmers, hunters, artisans, religious leaders, and warriors. Many lived in social systems far superior to the archaic, inbred monarchies of Western Europe.

The Hohokams of south-central Arizona built a great city with streets, plazas, and four-story apartment buildings, and they dug irrigation canals across the desert a thousand years before Columbus was born. Their artisans used fermented cactus juice to create

That's
Not
in My
American
History
Book

48

acid-etching works of art on seashells hundreds of years before European artists "invented" acid etching. Hohokam trade routes extended hundreds of miles, from the Gulf of Mexico to the Pacific Ocean.

While Europe was mired in the Dark Ages, the Mississippians built one of the largest cities in the world across the river from present-day St. Louis. Called Cahokia, it thrived for some 700 years. Built around 600 A.D., it was a walled city of five square miles containing more than a hundred ceremonial and temple mounds. Some 10,000 people lived within its walls and perhaps three times that number around them. The supreme ruler of the Mississippians lived in a temple atop an earthen mound more than ten stories high. The base of the mound was larger than any of the pyramids of Egypt or Mexico. Not until the turn of the nineteenth century did Philadelphia, then the largest city in the United States, finally reach a population equal to that of Cahokia and its surrounding settlements.

The island natives who greeted Columbus and his band no

Communal fishing in ancient America Many pre-Columbian Native Americans lived in societies far superior to those of Europe.

doubt were awed by the appearance of their visitors from the sea, but it is doubtful they felt threatened or intimidated by them. Physically, the Tiano towered over their European visitors. Thanks to a diet of berries, fruit, and fish, the average male Tiano stood nearly six feet tall. By contrast, the Latin voyagers who accompanied Columbus averaged about five feet three inches in height. Some of the Tiano elderly were in their seventies. Most Europeans of that era would not see fifty, the result of poor diets and recurring plagues that had swept the squalid cities of Europe for centuries. (Columbus, racked by arthritis and bent by old age, would be dead at fifty-six.)

Who were these natives of tan skin and gentle manner—these people Columbus called Indians? We know their ancestors migrated from Asia across the Bering Strait over many centuries. But we are still trying to unravel the mystery of when they came and how their cultures evolved. Those questions yet puzzle our anthropologists and archaeologists, and most perplexing of all is this book's next subject: the mystery of Poverty Point, the "New York City" of ancient America.

In the predawn, the great shaman was awakened to be dressed in his ceremonial garments. Accompanied by attendants and torch bearers, he proceeded across the courtyard and through the sleeping city. The procession moved along a wide thoroughfare until it came to the base of a great, shadowy mound rising out of a treeless plain and overlooking a river. As the attendants took their places at the base of the mound, the shaman climbed the steep steps to the apex. There, he waited. When the first ray of sunlight flashed above the treeline beyond the river and illuminated his face, he raised his arms and began to chant—thanking the spirits for sending the sun to watch over his people.

Far below, still in darkness, the inhabitants of the city began to emerge from their thatched homes. They stood, attentive, as sunlight slowly revealed the holy man atop the great mound. As his high-pitched chant echoed across the city, the sunlight moved steadily downward and the details of the mound took form. It emerged from the darkness as a giant earthen bird, more than 80 feet high and with a wingspan of more than 600 feet. After reciting their individual prayers, the residents could begin their daily routines, reassured they had been blessed for another day.

This ceremonial scenario did not take place in Central or South America. It took place in North America centuries before the emergence of the Inca, Aztec, and Maya. This ceremony, or one very much like it, took place almost a thousand years before there was a Rome, 1,600 years before the birth of Christ, even before the birth of Moses.

Between 1700 and 1600 B.C., a tribe of Native Americans constructed a remarkable city on a plain overlooking what was then the west fork of the Mississippi River in what is now northeast Louisiana. Even more remarkable than the city itself is the premise that it was built at a time when the inhabitants of North America were supposed to be hunters and gatherers living in small, nomadic clans. The builders of this great city are known today simply as the "Poverty Point Indians." Archaeologists named them that because the remains of their city rest upon the grounds of a nineteenth-century plantation named Poverty Point. It is an ignoble legacy for a proud people of amazing accomplishment.

It was a well-planned city, designed with geometric precision. It had a port, a marketplace, wide streets, a 37-acre plaza, and a drainage system. The residential area consisted of earthen terraces lain out in giant semicircles more than a mile in length. The terraces, built some 5 feet high and 50 feet across, provided both foundation and drainage system for row upon row of dwellings constructed of woven cane walls and thatched roofs. Dominating the city and visible for miles was the bird mound. It still soars more than 70 feet above the plain and might have been as tall as 80 to 100 feet before being exposed to 3,600 years of erosion.

Even more impressive than its height was the placement of the mound in relation to the city. Bisecting the city were several thoroughfares, one pointing to within a degree of the setting sun at its closest point in summer and another to within a degree of the setting sun at its furthermost point in winter. The mound sat between these roadways, the beak of the giant bird pointing to the position of the setting sun at the spring and autumn equinoxes. A tall post rose out of the central plaza, its foundation indicating that it might have stood 80 to 100 feet high. At the outer edge of the city, smaller posts in a semicircle measured the shadow cast by the post in the plaza. Amazingly, it appears the entire city was designed as a giant calendar.

Archaeologists have called Poverty Point "North America's New York City of its day." Indeed, it seems to have been a hub for cultural, religious, commercial, and artistic activity. It also was the hub of a loose-knit empire of people of similar culture stretching some 250 miles along the base of the Mississippi River Valley. Archaeologists believe Poverty Point was a center, not a capital. Its rulers did not attempt to subjugate outlying villages. It was an empire bound not by rule of force, but by a shared culture, commerce, and religious belief.

We still know little about the physical appearance of the inhabitants of Poverty Point. Limited excavations of nearby burial mounds have produced only a few remnants of bone. But those

That's
Not
in My
American
History
Book

who lived there left behind an abundance of artifacts, tools, and weapons that speak volumes. We know the Poverty Point natives were hard-working and prosperous. They were physically strong enough to carry woven cane baskets filled with 50 or more pounds of dirt, moving them several hundred yards from the barrow pits they dug to build their great mounds and miles of roads and terraces.

We know the Poverty Point natives were energetic, artistic, and intelligent. They constructed boats capable of long journeys and established trade routes that extended up the Mississippi River and its tributaries as far as present-day Wisconsin, east to Ohio, and west to Oklahoma. From these locations, they brought back stones—gray flint, quartz crystal, sandstone, hermatite, and magnetite. They traded for copper gleaned from the shores of Lake Superior by an advanced culture that inhabited that region. From the stones and copper, Poverty Point artisans chipped, buffed, and polished beautiful works of art. Thousands of small, delicate replicas of owls fashioned from stone have been recovered at the site, some bearing marks that could be the logo signatures of individual artists. From rare stones and copper, they fashioned fine jewelry. From the flint, they made tools and weapons.

The natives of Poverty Point did not cultivate crops, exploding the theory that herding and agriculture must accompany civilization. They had no need to grow crops or domesticate animals. The area abounded with berries, fruit, fish, and game. In pursuit of wild game, they developed weapons unique in North America at that time. One such device was a bolo used to capture birds and small animals. They refined a javelin that could be hurled great distances with accuracy with the aid of an ancient, sling-type device called an *atlatl*. They started fish farms in the barrow pits excavated to build their city.

Before each residence was a cooking pit. The natives did not cook with wood, but heated clay balls that retained and gave off radiant heat as they prepared food in what archaeologists describe as ancient "microwave ovens." The clay balls were of varying size and shape, designed to control the heat they produced. Many of the cooking balls bore symbols and marks, probably identifying them as belonging to certain households.

The lives of the residents of Poverty Point almost certainly revolved around religious activity. From atop the crown of the ceremonial mound, succeeding generations of religious leaders are believed to have conducted rites at sunrise and sunset at significant times of the year.

"This mound was not built simply to impress the inhabitants," said Jon Gibson, professor of archaeology at the University of Louisiana at Lafayette. "It was built to be viewed from above."

What is not known is whether it was built to be seen by the sun or an owl in flight or an unseen presence residing beyond the clouds who occasionally roared, cast bolts of light toward the earth, and sent wind and rain.

One can only imagine the wonder of Poverty Point residents each morning when the rising sun unveiled their bird mound. And it must have been an awe-inspiring sight when the sun set behind the mound, sending its shadow gliding slowly across the city, signaling the end of another day.

Archaeologists believe the Poverty Point culture thrived for

PART
ONE
*Nolichunky
Jack and
Patriotic
Horseflies*

53

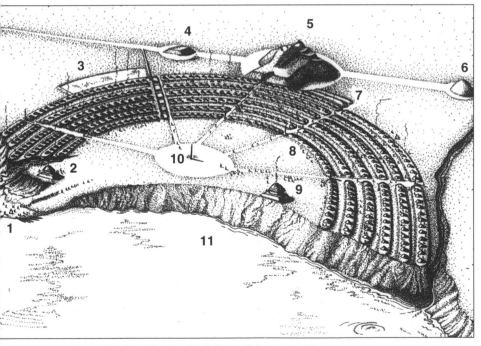

Ancient America's "New York City" Poverty Point as it would have appeared around 1350 B.C.: (1) boat landing; (2) marketplace; (3) barrow pit; (4) square mound; (5) giant bird mound; (6) burial mound; (7) thoroughfares; (8) thatched homes built on terraces; (9) plaza post used to measure seasons; (10) temple; (11) west fork of the Mississippi River.
Jon. L. Gibson, professor of archaeology at the University of Southwestern Louisiana

★

That's
Not
in My
American
History
Book

54

more than a thousand years before it ceased to exist around 500 B.C.—some 2,000 years before Columbus arrived in the Americas. The population of the city and surrounding settlements probably never exceeded 5,000—little more than a village by today's standards, but a megalopolis in its time.

The greatest mystery of Poverty Point is the design and construction of the city itself. It did not grow helter-skelter as cities are prone to do. No city in the United States today is as well planned or organized as was Poverty Point. Although small settlements grew around it, the city itself remained the same through the centuries. It appears to have been designed by a single individual at one point in time. Archaeologists believe the entire complex was built in one 20-year span, requiring millions of hours of labor. How an individual, or perhaps a group of leaders, could bring together thousands of people at that time and place and organize and inspire so large a workforce to complete such a monumental project is the greatest puzzle of all.

Archaeologists have only begun to scratch the surface at Poverty Point. The site was not even confirmed as a major archaeological find until the 1950s when aerial photographs revealed its scope. Currently, less than three percent of the site has been explored. But even as excavations continue, it becomes clear the Poverty Point natives left a legacy. From the Gulf Coast to Wisconsin, from the Carolinas to Texas, one can find thousands of ceremonial and burial mounds, no doubt built by succeeding generations of the descendants of these amazing people.

The Mysterious Death of Pocahontas

 The story of Pocahontas reads like a classic, romantic fairy tale. She was the beautiful daughter of a powerful Native American chief who saved the life of Capt. John Smith by shielding his body with her own. She also saved Jamestown, the first successful English settlement in the New World, by warning its inhabitants of an impending attack by her own people.

That is the legend.

The real story is much more fascinating than the cinematic and literary fiction that has distorted the life of this most interesting character in American history. And most intriguing of all is the mystery surrounding not her life, but her death.

Her native name was Natoaka, and she was the daughter of the leader of a confederation of Algonquin tribes that inhabited what is now the state of Virginia. The early English settlers, unable to pronounce the chief's name, named him Chief Powhatan because the tribes under his rule were called the Powhatans—itself, an English corruption.

In 1607, three ships carrying 105 Englishmen landed on the Virginia coastline. Two previous attempts by the English to colonize the New World had failed, but this venture was designed to succeed. It was well financed by London businessmen who, with the blessing of the Crown, had raised a large portion of the supporting funds by conducting a lottery. The men selected for the expedition were not ordinary settlers, but soldiers of fortune—military or ex-military men, heavily armed and well supplied.

Their mission was to build a fort and establish a trading outpost. The Spanish to the south had found gold and silver, and the French to the north had established a thriving fur trade with the natives. These Englishmen wanted to exploit this unknown territory and find treasure in whatever form it might appear.

Making their way inland on the James River, they constructed their fort, explored the nearby forest, and became acquainted with the natives. They named their settlement Jamestown. However, they were not prepared for the harsh winter that descended on them. Disease claimed half their number, and all might have died if the Powhatans had not come to their aid with food and native medicines.

As the Englishmen extended their explorations in a frustrated attempt to discover some kind of treasure in the wilderness, there were occasional clashes with the Powhatans. One of the leaders of the expedition, a veteran soldier named Captain John Smith, was exploring along the Chickahominy River when he came upon a band of native warriors and was taken prisoner. Legend has it that they were about to club him to death when a young girl ran for-

The baptism of Pocahontas Groomed to wed a Jamestown planter, the Indian princess was tutored in British customs and religion.

ward to cradle his head in her arms, saving his life. The girl was Natoaka.

Many historians doubt the accuracy of the story, because it was not recorded in Captain Smith's detailed personal journal about his adventures in America. Also, those who wonder if there was an ensuing romantic involvement will be disappointed to learn this probably was not the case. Natoaka was believed to be twelve years old at the time, and John Smith would have been twenty-nine. What apparently did happen was that the girl developed what might be described as an adolescent crush on the handsome visitor.

Whether because of her infatuation with Smith or simple curiosity about the strange people who had come to her land,

Pocahontas as Lady Rebecca This portrait is believed to have been painted in 1616, shortly before her death. *Virginia State Library*

That's
Not
in My
American
History
Book

Natoaka was a frequent visitor at Jamestown. The settlers gave her the name Pocahontas. On at least one occasion, when her father became angry at English transgressions and threatened an attack on Jamestown, Pocahontas risked her life to warn the inhabitants, possibly saving the settlement. Then in 1609, just two years after his arrival, John Smith returned to England. With his departure, Pocahontas no longer visited Jamestown.

Meanwhile, the Englishmen discovered their treasure. It was green gold, and it came to them in the form of a plant called *tobacco* grown by the natives. John Rolfe, a representative of the Virginia Company, which sponsored the expedition, sent the first shipment of cured tobacco to England. As European demand for the product grew, so did tensions between colonists and the Powhatans.

The scarcity of open land on which to grow tobacco was a continuing problem for Rolfe and the Jamestown planters. Dense forest blanketed the area. But within the forest were open fields belonging to the Indians. Over many generations, the Powhatans had felled and burned trees to create fields where they rotated crops of corn, squash, and beans. The Jamestown planters began confiscating unused fields to plant tobacco. Hostilities ensued; soon the English were chasing the Powhatans from their planted fields and finally from their villages, to utilize those sites for planting.

During a war between the planters and Powhatans in 1612, Pocahontas was taken captive by the Englishmen. When she inquired about the whereabouts of John Smith, she was informed by Rolfe that he had died in England. On Rolfe's instructions, Pocahontas was taken to Jamestown and never returned to her people. She was taught to read and write English, baptized, and given the Christian name Rebecca. It soon became apparent that Rolfe was grooming her for marriage. The ceremony took place in 1614, when she was eighteen years old. The marriage had the blessing of her father, and eight years of peace followed as a result of the union.

In 1616, Rebecca Rolfe accompanied her husband to England, where she was introduced to the King and Queen. Graceful, soft-spoken, and beautiful, she became the darling of London society, attending gala balls given in her honor. She was called Lady Rebecca.

When Rebecca gave birth to a son, the Rolfes moved from Bell Inn, near St. Paul Cathedral, to a large, elegant home owned by the Virginia Company in the quiet village of Brentwood, just west of London. It was there the fairy-tale life of the Indian princess turned tragic. She discovered that her husband had lied to her.

PART
ONE
*Nolichunky
Jack and
Patriotic
Horseflies*

59

From friends, Pocahontas learned that John Smith was not dead. In fact, he was living in a village nearby. She also learned that he was married and the father of several children. When Smith was informed of her presence at Brentwood, he went to visit her. This is how he described that meeting in his journal:

> Hearing she was at Brentwood with divers [several] of my friends, I went to see her. After a modest salutation, without any word, she turned about, obscured her face as not seeming well contented and in that humor . . . we all left her . . . repenting myself to have written instead.

From that day Lady Rebecca became reclusive, and her health seemed to fail her. She never left England. On the day she, her son Tom, and her husband boarded the ship that would return them to America, Lady Rebecca lapsed into a coma and died. She was buried at nearby Gravesend. She was believed to be twenty-one years old.

The very timing of her death casts a pall of suspicion over its circumstance. Did she die of a broken heart, having learned that the man she loved and thought dead was alive and married to another? Could she have taken her own life? Did she, as her husband explained, die of a mysterious fever on the very day of their scheduled departure? Was there a more sinister explanation? Could she have been murdered in a jealous rage?

The answers lie buried in an unmarked grave some twenty miles east of London in the cemetery of St. George's Church at Gravesend. However, on the banks of the River Thames in London, there stands a statue of the Indian princess and below it this tribute:

> *Gentle and humane, she was the friend of the
> earliest struggling English colonists whom
> she nobly rescued, protected and helped.*

John Rolfe returned to Virginia alone, leaving his infant son, Tom, in England in the care of an uncle. Tom Rolfe was twenty-five when he went to the land of his mother's birth. He married

That's
Not
in My
American
History
Book

and became the father of a daughter. From this grandchild of Pocahontas descended several prominent American families. Among her descendants was First Lady Edith Bolling Gault Wilson, wife of President Woodrow Wilson.

There is one final, tragic footnote to the story of the Indian princess who befriended the Jamestown settlers. In 1622, a bitter war ensued between the Powhatan tribes and Virginia settlers. By 1636, the tobacco planters of Jamestown had destroyed the last Powhatan village in the region, slaughtering those who could not escape. They burned the village and planted tobacco where it had stood.

PART TWO

The Midnight Ride of Sibyl Ludington

America's Forgotten Heroes

The pages of America's past are filled with the stories of larger-than-life heroes, and their monuments look down upon a thousand town squares. But where are the monuments to Elizabeth Freeman, James Beckwourth, Constantino Brumidi, and Jacob de Cardova? De Cardova, a Jamaican Jew, and Beckwourth, an African-American frontiersman, were far more instrumental in opening the great American West than were Kit Carson or William Cody. Brumidi, an Italian immigrant, literally sacrificed his life to leave the American people a priceless legacy; and Elizabeth Freeman, a slave, went to court and won her freedom almost eight decades before the Emancipation Proclamation. These are their stories— the heroes and heroines history forgot.

Leaving Paul Revere in the Dust

 Listen my children and you shall hear
Of the midnight ride of . . . Sibyl Ludington?
Ludington? That does not rhyme with *hear*. How about William Dawes or Israel Bissel? No, Dawes does not rhyme with much of anything. And who would ever believe there was a Revolutionary War hero named Bissel?

Paul Revere?

That's it! The midnight ride of Paul Revere!

Perhaps Henry Longfellow did not follow that logic when he penned his famous poem. Then again, perhaps he did because, whatever the source of his inspiration, it was not based on the reality of the events that transpired.

No one would dispute that Paul Revere was a patriot and an instrumental force in the American Revolution. But despite the poem that immortalized him, there is no evidence to suggest that he ever awakened a single minuteman.

The real hero of that famous ride was a 25-year-old mail carrier named Israel Bissel, who rode some 400 miles in five days, alerting local militias that a British force was marching on Lexington and Concord. Yet another noteworthy ride was accomplished by a 16-year-old girl named Sibyl Ludington, who rode more than 40 miles in six hours and called out an army of patriots to halt a British advance at Danbury, Connecticut. And there was the ride of Jack Jouett, who rode through the night to warn Governor Thomas Jefferson of Virginia of an impending attack on the temporary state capital at Charlottesville.

The famous midnight ride of Paul Revere? It was nothing more than poetic fiction from the pen and fertile imagination of a master storyteller.

It was never Revere's role to alert the militias. His mission that fateful night was to ride to Lexington and warn rebel leaders Samuel Adams and John Hancock that British soldiers were on the

That's
Not
in My
American
History
Book

64

way to arrest them. Revere also never saw those famous signal lanterns in the Old North Church tower that night. When the signal was given, he was on the other side of town. It made little difference, because the watchman gave the two-if-by-sea signal when he saw British soldiers climbing into boats. However, they rowed only a short distance before landing and going the remainder of the way on land.

On the eve of the historic skirmish between British soldiers and local militias at Lexington and Concord, Revere did ride to Lexington to alert Adams and Hancock. He was having a midnight snack with them when William Dawes arrived and suggested that

Midnight rider
Though numerous patriots warned of the approach of British forces, Paul Revere was not among them.
National Archives & Records Administration

he and Revere ride to Concord to warn the citizens there of the British advance.

Revere and Dawes were en route to Concord when they met Dr. Samuel Prescott, who was on his way to Lincoln. They joined Dr. Prescott and, upon their arrival in Lincoln, the doctor awakened Nathaniel Baker and suggested he alert local citizens that the British were coming. That was as close as Revere would come to living up to the legend.

As the trio rode toward Concord, they were met by six British soldiers. Dr. Prescott escaped, but Revere and Dawes were captured. Later that night, Dawes escaped and rode on to Concord without Revere. Questioned by his captors and faced with the possibility of being hanged for treason, Revere talked freely or, as historian Richard W. Odonnel once put it, "he blabbed everything." He at least satisfied his captors sufficiently for them to release him the following morning.

At about the time that Revere was being set free, the real hero of that famous ride mounted a horse at Watertown, Massachusetts. Israel Bissel was a slender rider for the mail service and a natural choice for the task at hand. He reined his mount south and thundered out of town to alert Colonial militias along the eastern

The real Revere
Captured along with Revere, William Dawes later escaped and continued on to Concord.
New-York Historical Society

seaboard of the British actions. Some three hours later he arrived in Worcester, 36 miles away—a remarkable ride considering that 30 miles a day was the norm for a traveler on horseback.

At Worcester, Bissel acquired a fresh mount and galloped through Pomfret and on to Brooklyn, Connecticut. From Brooklyn he headed toward New Haven. He rode day and night, pausing only for rest and nourishment. He continued through Stratford and Greenwich, Connecticut, and on to New York. There he rested for a time before riding to Brunswick, New Jersey. From

⭐

**That's
Not
in My
American
History
Book**

66

there he galloped off toward Philadelphia, where the ride finally ended.

In 118 hours, Israel Bissel traveled more than 400 miles, stopping in hamlets as well as cities to alert the militias. Following the clashes between minutemen and redcoats at Lexington and Concord, Colonial forces converged at Breed's Hill to repel the British. Bissel became a hero, but with time, the story of his deeds faded from memory.

Like Bissel, others became local heroes for completing remarkable rides. When Lord Cornwallis invaded Virginia in 1781 with 5,000 British troops, he devised a plan to trap and capture Governor Jefferson and the Virginia General Assembly. Cornwallis dispatched Col. Banastre Tarleton with a large force for a surprise attack on the temporary state capital at Charlottesville. Colonists discovered the plan when British troops were heard passing Cuckoo's Tavern in the night. Jack Jouett ran to the stable to saddle a fast horse and rode through the night to warn the governor, allowing Jefferson and his fellow lawmakers to escape capture.

A teenage girl named Sibyl Ludington accomplished yet another remarkable ride. It took place on the night of April 27, 1777, after a messenger arrived at her father's farm to inform him British troops had burned Danbury and were advancing on Long Island Sound. Sibyl's father, a captain of the local militia, could not leave his command, so he summoned his daughter and instructed her to call out the area farmers to fight.

He boosted her into the saddle and handed her a stick. She raced through the night, pausing at each farmhouse to crash the stick against the door and shout: "The British are coming! Fall out and fight!"

By morning's light, she had covered 40 miles in six hours, stopping at scores of houses along the way. And she had called out enough men to repel the British. For her amazing ride, Sibyl Ludington became a local heroine. Then, like Bissel and Jouett, she was forgotten with the passing of time.

More than half a century after those momentous events, Longfellow penned his famous poem. As a result, a mantle of fame settled on the shoulders of a Boston silversmith named Paul Revere. In the minds of future generations, he became that lone rider in the night, calling a nation to arms. And *The Midnight Ride of Paul Revere* assured Henry Wadsworth Longfellow a place in history as well, as one of our nation's greatest poets.

Heroines of the Battlefield

A classic dispatch written by Union Army Col. Elijah H. C. Cavins during the U.S. Civil War is revealing in its simplicity:

A corporal was promoted to sergeant for gallant conduct in the Battle of Fredericksburg, since which time the sergeant has become the mother of a child.

Even as debate continues on the role of female soldiers in combat, it is a little-known fact that hundreds of women already have fought, and many have died, in our nation's wars. In fact, women fought in America's wars even before the existence of the United States.

It was not at all unusual to see women on the battlefield during the American Revolution. In the Civil War, almost 400 women posed as men to join the Union and Confederate armies—and those are only the ones we know about. Many more female enlistees, who posed as men to join the armies of North and South, probably lie in military cemeteries beneath headstones bearing their male aliases.

If Margaret Corbin could be transported through time, she might provide some insight into the continuing debate on women in combat. When her husband joined the Continental Army in 1776, she accompanied him as a camp follower, a common practice back then. The women of that era labored beside their husbands in the fields, loaded muskets during attacks by Indians, and frequently accompanied their husbands when they marched off to war.

At the Battle of Fort Washington in 1776, a devastating British artillery barrage rained down on the Colonial forces. Margaret Corbin clung to the breastworks as the earth shook around her. When the bombardment subsided and the smoke began to clear, she became aware of the devastation around her. She ran to her

That's
Not
in My
American
History
Book

68

husband's cannon and found his body lying there among the debris. Tears streaming down her face, she stepped up and fired his cannon. Then, she began reloading it.

Inspired by her bravery, artillerymen along the line lifted themselves from the rubble, straightened their weapons, and joined in the battle. An incoming cannonball felled Margaret Corbin. Severely wounded, she remained an invalid for the rest of her life. When she died, she was buried with full military honors at West Point.

Deborah Gannett was another Revolutionary War heroine. Disguising herself as a man, she enlisted in the Continental Army and distinguished herself in combat. But her military career ended when she was wounded at Tarrytown, New York, and her secret became known. Following the war, she became the first American woman to go on the lecture circuit. After her death, Congress voted to give her husband a pension as the surviving spouse of a Continental soldier.

Molly Pitcher The female camp followers of the Revolutionary War became known as Molly Pitchers. *National Archives & Records Administration*

Mary Hays also distinguished herself on the battlefield. At the Battle of Monmouth in June of 1778, she raced through a hail of gunfire to get ammunition for the men in the ranks. As she ran, a cannonball ripped away part of her dress, barely missing her legs. Ignoring the close call, she grabbed shot and powder and ran back to the line. A loud cheer went up from the soldiers, who recognized true heroism when they saw it.

⭐
PART
TWO
*The
Midnight
Ride of
Sibyl
Ludington*

69

There are many long-forgotten stories of women who played roles in the struggle for American independence. They served as field nurses, loaded weapons during battle, cooked, mended uniforms, carried water to cool cannons and parched throats, and when it became necessary, they fought. And, in spite of the Betsy Ross myth, it is believed the women at Fort Schuyler, New York, made the first stars-and-stripes flag from assorted garments and flew it in defiance of the British.

The camp followers of that era were called Molly Pitchers. Contrary to legend, Molly Pitcher was not a real person; the name symbolized all women who accompanied the Continental Army. Sadly, historians generally ignored their exploits. In 1840 Charles Francis Adams, the grandson of President John Adams, finally began paying long-overdue tribute to their contributions. Upon learning of their deeds, he went on the lecture circuit, telling their stories.

"It is unfortunate," he noted in his writings, "that the heroism of the females of the Revolution has gone from memory with the generation that witnessed it."

☞   ☞   ☞

The Civil War had its female camp followers, but it also saw an extraordinary number of women who managed to fool recruiters by disguising themselves as men and enlisting in the armies on both sides. Apparently, it was not that difficult to deceive recruiters. Physical examinations were spotty at best. About all that was required of an enlistee was an operative trigger finger and two opposing teeth strong enough to rip open the paper containing a minie ball cartridge.

Sarah Emma Evelyn Edmonds, a Canadian, posed as "Franklin Thompson" to join the 2nd Michigan Volunteers. She feared the prospect of undergoing a physical examination when she reported for duty, but as it turned out, she had nothing to

That's

Not

in My

American

History

Book

worry about. In her memoirs, titled *Nurse and Spy*, she described her examination: "It consisted of a firm handshake."

Although her secret was later discovered, she remained in the service. She served as a nurse and then as a spy, completing several dangerous intelligence missions behind Confederate lines.

Women joined the armies of North and South—actually, more North than South—for many reasons. So many smooth-faced boys filled the ranks of both armies that it was relatively easy for a girl to pass herself off as an adolescent male. There were strong feelings for "the cause" on both sides, and the desire to fight was not exclusive to the male population. Many joined for financial reasons; it was the only way a young girl could earn her own money. More often, the army provided a means for a young girl to escape the drudgery of farm life and seek adventure in far-off and exotic places.

That was the motivation for Sarah Rosetta Wakeman to cut her hair, bind her breasts, and enlist in the 153rd Regiment of the New York State Volunteers. She did so under the name of Lyons Wakeman. Her story, based on a collection of her letters, has been chronicled by Civil War historian Lauren Cook Burgess, editor of *The Uncommon Soldier*. Wakeman was sent to New Orleans, which did not appear particularly exotic under Union occupation when she arrived there in 1863. Nor did the swamps and marshlands of south Louisiana seem particularly exotic when clouds of disease-spreading mosquitoes descended on campsites. In June of 1863, she wrote to her parents:

> I am well and tough as a bear. I have got so that I can drill just as well as any man there is in my regiment.

That August she wrote:

> I don't feel afraid to go [into battle]. I don't believe there are any Rebel bullets made for me yet . . . But if it is God's will for me to fall in the field of battle, it is my will to go and never return home.

With the opening of Gen. Nathaniel Banks's Red River Campaign in the spring of 1864, Rosetta Wakeman marched some 300 miles through the swamplands and wilderness backroads of Louisiana. She fought in several engagements before being exposed to the horrors of major warfare. At Mansfield, Louisiana,

Sister against sister
Rosetta Wakeman, a farm girl, posed as a man to join the 153rd New York during the Civil War. *Mansfield Civil War Museum*

Union forces suffered a terrible defeat. They regrouped at Pleasant Hill and fought the Confederates to a draw before being forced to retreat once more, fleeing south under constant harassment by Confederate cavalry. Finally, Louisiana's semitropical weather, stagnant bayou waters, and the meager rations Rosetta Wakeman had to share with her comrades did what no rebel bullet could accomplish. She died of dysentery.

Rosetta Wakeman had been devoted to her family. Aware that her father was deeply in debt, she sent most of her army pay back home to Afton, New York, to keep the farm going. In one letter she wrote: "I knew that I could help you more to leave home than to stay there with you." However, her parents were embarrassed by the actions of their daughter. For years they told their younger children that Lyons Wakeman was an older brother. It was only when a sister found her letters and a photograph in the attic that the family secret was revealed.

Today, Rosetta Wakeman rests beneath a military headstone at Chalmette National Cemetery in St. Bernard Parish, Louisiana—

★

That's
Not
in My
American
History
Book

72

a world away from the home and family she loved. The headstone reads simply: "4006 Lyons Wakeman, N.Y."

Many women who posed as men in the Union Army managed to keep their true identities secret throughout the war. Albert D. J. Cashier served with distinction in the Vicksburg campaign as a member of an Illinois regiment. Years later, when "he" was hospitalized as a war veteran, doctors discovered that their patient was really Jennie Hodges.

After a great deal of debate, the Union Pension Bureau allowed Hodges to continue receiving her army pension. She later entered a soldier's home, but only after she agreed to wear a dress and call herself Jennie instead of Albert.

Rose Rooney, on the other hand, did not have to pose as a man to join the Confederate Army. She openly signed on as a female enlistee in the Crescent Blues Volunteers at New Orleans in 1861. Her designated duty was to serve as cook and laundress for the company. The men saw nothing wrong with this arrangement and welcomed her as a member of the unit, which eventually became Company K of the 15th Louisiana Infantry. She accompanied the men to Virginia, and it was there her role abruptly changed.

As the First Battle of Bull Run raged, and the outcome was still in doubt, she ran through a field of heavy fire to tear down a rail fence, allowing a battery of Confederate artillery to race through in time to stop a Union charge. Her heroic act was credited with turning the tide in that sector of the battlefield.

Rose Rooney served in Robert E. Lee's Army of Northern Virginia for four years and fought in many battles. She was still in the ranks when Lee surrendered at Appomattox in 1865.

It was more than a century later, in 1989, when historian Lauren Cook Burgess dressed herself in a Union Army uniform to participate in a reenactment of the Battle of Antietam at Sharpsburg, Maryland. National Park Service authorities saw her coming out of a ladies room and stopped her. They prohibited her from participating, pointing out that they wanted to preserve the authenticity of the battle. Unwittingly, they had picked on the wrong soldier.

Burgess sued the National Park Service for discrimination. In court she proved that no less than five women posing as men had fought at Antietam. Two of them were wounded and one was killed. She won her case.

The Unsung Pathfinder

A man has to be spoiling for a fight to ride a horse 2,000 miles through the wilderness just to find one. If he then rides another 3,000 miles to fight in yet another war, he must be James Beckwourth.

Names like Kit Carson, Buffalo Bill Cody, and Davy Crockett are familiar to all. They were the stuff of legend—dashing frontiersmen galloping across the plains, blazing trails into the wilderness, fighting to the death at the Alamo. But none of them came close to equaling the adventurous life of James Pierson Beckwourth. While imaginative writers back east fictionalized the exploits of our better known frontier heroes, Beckwourth was living those great adventures. The fact that his story is missing from that colorful chapter of our history is a terrible oversight by our historians.

Beckwourth was born in Fredericksburg, Virginia, in 1798. When James was only thirteen, his father apprenticed him to a blacksmith who took him to St. Louis. Although his mentor was a good craftsman who taught Beckwourth well, the blacksmith also was an ill-tempered tyrant who often abused the boy. At age eighteen, following an altercation with his boss, Beckwourth ran away. Restless by nature, he spent several years traveling from town to town, working as an itinerant blacksmith rather than settling down. During that time he met a succession of grizzled frontiersmen, who related stories about an amazing land to the west where great mountains rose out of the plains. Beckwourth marveled at their stories and decided he must see those mountains for himself. He was twenty-five when the opportunity to fulfill that dream presented itself.

Beckwourth received word that Gen. William Henry Ashley was forming a wilderness expedition for the Rocky Mountain Fur Trading Company and was determined to join it. Although

That's
Not
in My
American
History
Book

Beckwourth had no experience as a frontiersman, his persistence impressed the organizers sufficiently for them to hire him.

In 1823 the expedition left St. Louis. Only seventeen years earlier, Meriwether Lewis and William Clark had completed their famous journey across the continent's outback, and John C. Fremont, who would become the self-proclaimed "Pathfinder of the American West," was a mere ten years old.

Beckwourth and his companions spent two years trapping, exploring, and mapping the continent from the Rocky Mountains to the Missouri River, experiencing many adventures along the way. When the expedition terminated in 1825, Beckwourth decided not to return to St. Louis with the others. He chose instead to live with the nomadic Crow Indians, who adopted him and gave him the name "Bull's Robe."

Beckwourth quickly earned a reputation as a great hunter. He became a fierce warrior, distinguishing himself in battles against rival tribes. His tribe elevated him to the status of war chief, and he became a legend among the Crow, who believed that he possessed supernatural powers.

He lived with the Crow for 12 years but in 1837, at age thirty-nine, he decided to return to white civilization and settle down. He took a wife and established a trading post in Colorado. But the wanderlust and desire for adventure inherent in Beckwourth's soul would not allow him to settle down. The prospect of danger seemed to draw him like a magnet.

Adventurers and explorers sought him out to lead them on expeditions into the wilderness. In 1842, Beckwourth traveled from Colorado to Georgia to fight in the Seminole Wars. Incredibly, he then re-crossed the continent to fight in the California Revolution that helped establish a republic there. Along the way, he met John C. Fremont and became his chief scout. It was Beckwourth who found the paths traveled by the famous "Pathfinder."

In 1850 Beckwourth made a discovery that should have secured a place for him in the forefront of American frontier history. A few miles northwest of what is now Reno, Nevada, he found a pass through the rugged Sierra Nevada Mountains. With the discovery, it was as if he had turned the key that unlocked the door to California.

He led the very first wagon train through Beckwourth Pass, and it was followed by a steady stream of humanity: adventurers lured by the prospect of becoming wealthy in the California gold fields

Lost frontier legend
James Beckwourth discovered a pass through the Sierra Nevada Mountains. *Mercaldo Archives*

and farmers seeking fertile lands. Within a few years, the Western Pacific Railroad would lay tracks through Beckwourth Pass, linking East and West.

In 1866, at age sixty-eight, Beckwourth took up arms for the final time when he became a scout in the Colorado Indian wars. The brutality of the Colorado Militia in subduing the Cheyenne and Arapaho tribes disturbed him, and he vowed to have no part in such future hostilities. He returned to his home near Denver, determined to live out the remainder of his life in peace. He had been there only a short time when a delegation of Crow chieftains visited him.

The Crow leaders told him their people were suffering, and their nation was in decline. They urged him to join them once more and use the powers they attributed to him to lead the Crow back to greatness. When Beckwourth declined, the chieftains insisted that he at least accept an invitation to a farewell feast in his honor at their encampment. He graciously accepted and accompanied them to the camp.

That night, Beckwourth became violently ill, suffering convulsions and a burning fever. He died the following day. The cause of

That's
Not
in My
American
History
Book

his death remains a mystery, but legend has it that the Crow chieftains poisoned him to keep his powerful spirit with them forever.

Many years later, a western historian wrote of Beckwourth: "Probably no man ever lived who met more personal adventure involving danger to [his] life."

By far, the most important thing Beckwourth did was to unlock the door to California with his discovery of Beckwourth Pass. Yet, even now, few students of history are aware of this contribution to the development of the American West.

Fewer still are aware that James Pierson Beckwourth was an African-American.

America's Michelangelo

 If you were to enter the great rotunda of our nation's Capitol building and look upward, you would be instantly awed by a magnificent work of art on the domed ceiling, 180 feet above. The initial reaction is to ask, "how?" How did the artist do it?

The painting, titled *Apotheosis of Washington,* is a work of incredible scope and artistry. It covers 4,664 square feet inside the concave surface of the dome. Light filtering through windows around the dome illuminates the colors, seeming to bring the figures to life.

At the focal point of the work, George Washington sits between figures representing Liberty and Victory. They are flanked by an inner circle of figures representing the thirteen original colonies. Around them, scenes depict the nation at work in the arts, science, commerce, industry, and agriculture. And in the forefront protecting them all is Freedom, a sword-wielding woman with a star-studded crown and striped shield.

Many Americans, having never visited the capital, are unaware of the existence of this masterful work. Fewer still have heard of its creator, a slightly built Italian immigrant with a fiery temperament and an enormous talent. His name is Constantino Brumidi, and his story is one of love and sacrifice for his adopted land—the United States of America.

A famous artist in his native Italy long before he came to America, Brumidi was almost fifty years of age when he fled Rome to escape political persecution. Upon visiting Washington and viewing the empty walls and ceilings of the United States Capitol building for the first time, he was seized by an irrepressible passion to fill them with paintings depicting the American story. He dedicated the final twenty-five years of his life to fulfilling that mission.

Brumidi was born in Rome in 1805. His artistic talents became obvious when he was a child, and upon reaching his teens, he en-

That's
Not
in My
American
History
Book

rolled in the Academy of Arts in Rome. By his mid-twenties, he had gained fame as one of Italy's leading artists. In fact, his reputation earned him a commission to restore works of art in the Vatican—a responsibility rarely entrusted to one so young.

By age thirty, Brumidi was recognized as Italy's greatest living fresco painter, following the tradition of Michelangelo Buonarroti and Leonardo da Vinci. Fresco painting is a demanding, laborious method of producing lasting works of art. It involves mixing colors with plaster, which is then troweled onto a ceiling or wall to create the artwork.

Unfortunately for Brumidi, he possessed strong political convictions as well as the temperament of an artist. That combination kept him in constant conflict with the church and Italian government. By the early 1850s, the conflicts had escalated to such a point that Brumidi had to flee Italy or face imprisonment.

Upon his arrival in America, he found a vibrant, rapidly growing nation that seemed far more obsessed with commerce and industry than the arts. At first the little artist from Italy, with his tousled hair and scraggly beard, did not attract a great deal of attention in Washington. But that would change. He was fifty-nine years old when he was commissioned to paint the rotunda dome in the Capitol building.

Brumidi had scaffolds erected 180 feet above the rotunda floor. There, lying on his back on scaffold boards only inches from the ceiling, he began applying colored plaster to the surface. He often worked day and night, for fresco painting is a technique that requires intense dedication from the artist. Chemical changes in the plaster add beauty and permanence to the work but also require the artist to work for extended periods without a break. Those parts of the artwork not completed before the plaster dries must be scraped off and redone.

Week after week, Brumidi troweled his plaster overhead while his shoulders and arms ached. It required eleven months to complete the work. When the scaffolds came down and the work was unveiled before an awestruck audience, Brumidi became famous overnight. He was bombarded by offers for other commissions. Had he accepted those offers, he could have become a wealthy man. But he had other plans.

"My one ambition," he wrote to a friend, "is that I may live long enough to make beautiful the Capital of the one country on earth in which there is liberty."

The work on the rotunda dome exacted a terrible physical toll

★

**PART
TWO**
*The
Midnight
Ride of
Sibyl
Ludington*

79

Our forgotten Michelangelo Constantino Brumidi dedicated his talents to decorating the nation's capital. *Library of Congress*

from Brumidi. Yet, he spent the next several years decorating the Capitol with magnificent works of art. Then in 1877, at age seventy-two, he took on another Herculean challenge. He set his scaffolds 60 feet above the rotunda floor where a blank wall, 8 feet high and 300 feet around the interior of the rotunda, awaited him. For years he had been planning a work to fill this space—a panoramic frieze composed of panels depicting scenes from American history.

For two years Brumidi worked like a man possessed, racing against time and age to complete the project. During that time he completed six panels, covering about one third of the surface. While working on the seventh panel, showing William Penn signing his treaty with the Indians, Brumidi lost his balance. As he was falling, he managed to grab a section of the scaffold. Clinging to it,

⭐

That's

Not

in My

American

History

Book

80

he dangled there, the equivalent of five stories above the rotunda floor. Several minutes passed before rescuers were able to reach him. There is little doubt the ordeal hastened his death a few months later.

Upon Brumidi's death, Congress commissioned his pupil, Filippo Costaggini, to complete the frieze. Costaggini spent the next eight years translating Brumidi's sketches into the masterful work seen on the wall of the rotunda today. However, there was more wall than there were Brumidi sketches. A thirty-foot section remained blank until 1953, when New York artist Allyn Cox completed the final panel.

Constantino Brumidi labored from 1855 to 1880 to cover the interior of the nation's Capitol with distinctive designs and beautiful paintings. During that time, he turned down commissions worth hundreds of thousands of dollars. The most he ever received was $3,200 per year, but the works he left are beyond price.

Today visitors to the Capitol can marvel at the legacy he left us. And if one looks closely, the signature of the artist may be found on some of the works. It is always the same: "C. Brumidi, artist. Citizen of the U.S."

Monitor vs. Virginia
The Story behind the Ironclads

Stephen R. Mallory, a visionary who loved the United States Navy, was assigned the job of destroying it. John Ericsson, an ill-tempered eccentric who hated the United States Navy, was the only man who could save it. Theirs was one of the most remarkable role reversals in history. But between them, Stephen Mallory and John Ericsson changed naval warfare forever.

Civil War buffs know well the story of the famous battle between the *Monitor* and the *Virginia*. Less well known is the story behind that legendary confrontation and the men who made it happen.

At the outbreak of the Civil War, the Confederacy formed a Department of the Navy, but the assortment of commercial vessels converted to warships under its command could hardly be called a navy. In fact, the department's greatest asset was not its fleet but its Secretary of the Navy—Stephen Mallory. Knowing that he could never match the United States Navy in ships or experienced officers, Mallory envisioned a small fleet of invincible, ironclad vessels roaming the seas, shells bouncing harmlessly from their sides as they steamed forward to splinter the Union's armada of wooden vessels.

It was not a new vision for Mallory. Before secession of the Southern states, he had been a respected member of the U.S. Senate, and as chairman of the Senate Commission on Naval Affairs, he spent years trying to convince his fellow lawmakers to build a U.S. flotilla of ironclad warships. His pleas fell on deaf ears. New England's shipbuilding industry, which wielded considerable influence in Washington, balked at the idea of retooling its shipyards to accommodate Mallory's proposal. But those lawmakers who had come to view Mallory as something of a fanatic on the subject later would regret that they did not listen to him.

⭐

That's
Not
in My
American
History
Book

With the formation of a Confederate government at Montgomery, Alabama, Mallory resigned from the U. S. Senate. Confederate President Jefferson Davis promptly appointed him Secretary of the Navy. Although Davis had doubts about Mallory's plan to build a fleet of iron-plated ships, he gave him permission to proceed. However, he did not provide Mallory with the resources necessary to accomplish his goal.

For his first ship, Mallory selected a steam frigate named the *Merrimac*. Its hull sat in the harbor at Norfolk, Virginia, where it had been scuttled when the Union Army abandoned the city. Under Mallory's direction, workmen began bolting thick metal plates to the wooden hull.

In the early months of the war, Washington, D.C., was awash

Mastermind behind the Monitor John Ericsson created a craft capable of countering the South's ironclad.
Dictionary of American Portraits

Clash of the ironclads

with wild rumors of Confederate activities at Norfolk. Union intelligence sources quickly confirmed the rumors. The Confederates were building a great iron monster capable of destroying any ship in the U.S. fleet. The news sent shock waves through Washington officialdom, because they had no doubt that Stephen Mallory was capable of building such a craft.

Gustavus Fox, assistant secretary of the U.S. Navy, posed the question on everyone's mind:

> Who is to prevent her [the *Merrimac*] from dropping anchor in the Potomac and throwing her hundred pound shells into the city . . . or battering down the walls of the Capital itself?

U.S. Secretary of War Edwin Stanton warned those gathered for a White House cabinet meeting: "She will lay all the cities of the seaboard under contribution." Of utmost concern was that the *Merrimac* would be capable of breaking any blockade of a Southern port—and the blockade constituted a major part of Union strategy for winning the war.

The USS *Monitor* and CSS *Virginia* slug it out in a landmark naval battle. *National Archives & Records Administration*

Father of the Virginia Stephen Mallory planned to create a fleet of invincible, iron-plated warships. *National Archives & Records Administration*

Following intense discussion, U.S. leaders concluded that only one man possessed the capabilities to design a warship to contend with the *Merrimac*: John Ericsson. He was the "Dr. Strangelove" of his day—vain, arrogant, and brilliant, the stereotypical eccentric scientist. Born in Sweden, he had immigrated to the United States and earned a reputation as something of a genius. But there was a

★

That's
Not
in My
American
History
Book

problem with Ericsson. He hated the U.S. Navy. Likewise, the Navy brass were not especially fond of him.

The Navy's disaffection with Ericsson was understandable. Sixteen years earlier, one of his experimental weapons had blown up, killing the U.S. Secretary of the Navy along with the U.S. Secretary of State and four other onlookers. The incident took place in 1845 as Ericsson demonstrated a new propeller-driven warship. During the exhibition, a gun exploded, claiming the aforementioned lives. Undaunted, Ericsson sent the Navy a bill for his work. The Navy refused to pay, and the ensuing feud lasted sixteen years.

U.S. Secretary of the Navy Gideon Welles finally volunteered to call on the inventor to ask him if he could build a warship capable of stopping the *Merrimac*. Upon meeting with Ericsson, Welles stressed that the very survival of the nation might depend on him. Ericsson informed Welles he would attempt to build such a warship, but only if he had President Lincoln's personal assurance that he would have complete control of the project. Armed with that assurance, Ericsson went to his drawing board and came away with the most unusual design for a warship ever devised until that time.

Ericsson's ship would not be iron-plated, but constructed entirely of metal. He included only two guns in his design. They were to be mounted in a revolving turret atop a watertight hull that sat barely above the water level.

When Navy officials saw the drawings, they panicked. There had never been such a vessel. They insisted it was madness to build a ship with only two guns, but even that objection paled in comparison to a more fundamental concern. They were convinced it would sink like a rock the moment it was launched.

Ericsson ignored the experts and assured Lincoln the vessel not only would float, it would be virtually unsinkable. In a letter to the president he noted: "The sea will ride over her and she shall live in it like a duck." Having reached the proverbial point of no return, Lincoln reluctantly allowed the project to proceed.

At a launch ramp on Manhattan's East River, construction began with Ericsson overseeing every detail. Meanwhile, 400 miles away at Norfolk, work on the *Merrimac* continued, hampered by limited funds and materials.

On January 30, 1862, the long-awaited launching of Ericsson's strange warship took place. It slid down the ramp into the river and, just as he had predicted, floated like a duck. From the completion of his design until launch, Ericsson had built his ship in just

101 days. He christened her the *Monitor*. In Norfolk, the Confederates were still a month away from completing work on the *Merrimac*.

No one had ever seen anything like the *Monitor*. It had forty-seven newly patented devices. One witness noted: "It looks like a cheese box sitting on a shingle." The crewmen of the *Monitor* soon learned, to their dismay, that the vessel navigated somewhat like a cheese box on a shingle. They experienced great difficulty just getting it out of the harbor and down the river. However, once in the open sea they were able to point it south and hold it on a fairly steady course for the 400-mile trip to Hampton Roads, Virginia. The *Monitor*, they discovered, was painfully slow and plagued with problems. Freezing water sometimes spilled through the gun turret, soaking the crew. The ventilators often malfunctioned, allowing fumes to overcome the men inside.

On March 8, 1862, the newly completed *Merrimac*, by then renamed the *Virginia*, came out of the bay at Hampton Roads to attack the Union fleet blockading the waterway. She headed straight for the Union sloop *Cumberland*, the most powerful warship in the federal fleet. The *Cumberland* opened fire on the ironclad, but as a Union officer later wrote: "The shot bounced off her like India rubber balls." The *Virginia* rammed the *Cumberland*, sinking her. She then turned on the Union ship *Congress*, setting it on fire, and went after the *Minnesota*. In attempting to escape, the *Minnesota* ran aground.

Into the chaos of this orgy of destruction steamed the most unusual vessel the Confederate crewmen had ever seen. It appeared to be a giant iron gun turret sitting almost at water level. The two vessels began firing at each other, with little effect. Finally, the *Monitor* retired from the action to replenish its supply of ammunition. It returned to action then retreated once more, when Capt. John L. Worden, temporarily blinded by steel fragments, had to be replaced as commander. Thinking he had won the battle, Capt. Catesby Jones of the *Virginia* withdrew to replenish ammunition and check for damage to his vessel. He intended to return the following morning and finish off the *Minnesota*.

The *Virginia* captain had reason to be confident. In one afternoon, Stephen Mallory's iron-plated warship had made a shambles of the Union fleet blockading Hampton Roads. But that night the *Monitor* anchored beside the *Minnesota*, prepared to defend her the following day.

★

That's
Not
in My
American
History
Book

On March 9, as the *Virginia* approached the *Minnesota*, crewmen were surprised to find the *Monitor* still on the scene. Captain Jones attacked, expecting to quickly sink the smaller vessel. The battle lasted four-and-a-half hours. Hull to hull, the iron monsters hammered at each other, unable to inflict serious damage. They fought at such close quarters their hulls repeatedly collided. Finally, the *Virginia* withdrew and returned to its Norfolk dock, leaving the bay to the *Monitor*.

Other than Captain Worden, the federals sustained only two injuries in the battle. Two *Monitor* crewmen were standing against the turret when it was struck by a shell. They were so disoriented by the ringing in their heads, they had to temporarily retire from the battle.

The iron warships did not meet again. Two months later, as Union troops approached Norfolk, the Confederates blew up the *Virginia* rather than let her fall into enemy hands. Ten months later, the *Monitor* sank in a storm off Cape Hatteras, North Carolina. Meanwhile, Northern shipyards built more iron warships and bolted metal plating to their wooden vessels.

As word of the great battle spread around the world, foreign leaders everywhere became concerned. Overnight, every other warship on the planet had become obsolete. The following observation appeared in a London newspaper: "About a week ago, the British discovered that their whole wooden navy was useless."

A Southern politician with a vision and an eccentric inventor with a magic drawing board had changed naval warfare forever. And John Ericsson, the man who hated the U.S. Navy, had succeeded in saving it.

Bet Freeman's Walk to Freedom

When Theodore Sedgwick answered the timid knock on his door at Sheffield, Massachusetts, that summer morning in 1781, he was surprised to find Bet Freeman standing there, a satchel at her side and her child cradled in her arms. Bet Freeman was a slave in the household of his friend, Col. John Ashley. Sedgwick, a prominent lawyer, had seen her there many times during his visits to the Ashley home. He was puzzled by her sudden appearance at his door and even more baffled by the strange look in her eyes.

"Why, Bet," he said, "what are you doing here?"

"I want you to go to the law and make me free," was her reply.

☞   ☞   ☞

The slavery issue might have been resolved and a Civil War averted if our forefathers had pursued a legal precedent established in the little-known Massachusetts trial of *Freeman vs. Ashley* that took place eighty-two years before the Emancipation Proclamation.

The plaintiff in that unusual case was Elizabeth Freeman, the slave who knocked on Theodore Sedgwick's door that morning. At stake was the legal question of whether, as stated in the new Massachusetts Constitution, "All men are born free and equal."

Until that day, Elizabeth Freeman had never known freedom. She also had never known her parents. She and her sister, Lizzie, were infants when they were purchased as slaves by Col. John Ashley of Ashley Falls, Massachusetts. A man of strong character and conviction, the colonel had a reputation for being kind to his slaves. Upon reaching her teen years, Bet, as Elizabeth was called, became a servant in the colonel's household. She later married another Ashley slave and was dismayed when her husband left home

★

That's
Not
in My
American
History
Book

to become a soldier in the Continental Army. During his absence she gave birth to a child, but her joy turned to grief upon learning that her husband had been killed in a battle. Overnight, she was a widow with a small child.

Colonel Ashley was politically influential in western Massachusetts in the years prior to and during the Revolutionary War. Because of his standing in the community, his home became a gathering place for similar men of influence, who engaged in political discussion while seated around a large table in the Ashley study. Bet Freeman, the serving girl, often overheard the men at the table talking about "freedom" and "equality" and "the inalienable rights of men."

One day in 1780, the leaders of the community gathered in the Ashley study to discuss ratification of the new Constitution of Massachusetts. Sedgwick was among those attending.

Before the tragedy of losing her husband, Bet Freeman had enjoyed such occasions. There was always a great deal of excitement in the house when the colonel's friends gathered, and both their discussions and the passion of their arguments fascinated Bet. She frequently lingered outside the study door to listen. On this occasion, while serving food and drinks to the guests, she overheard the colonel reading from a paper. One phrase in particular captured her attention:

" . . . All men are born free and equal."

In the days that followed, Bet could not get the words out of her mind. Finally, she found the courage to ask Colonel Ashley if the words on the paper meant that she was going to be free. He patiently explained to her that the words did not apply to slaves.

Bet Freeman realized the colonel was a very smart man who, surely, knew about such things. She had never questioned his wisdom or authority. Still, she could not get the words out of her mind. She had been told that the soldiers were away fighting for freedom. If that was true, she reasoned, her husband had been a soldier and he had died fighting for freedom. How then could she and her child be denied the freedom he had earned for them? Could it be possible the colonel was wrong? She had to know the answer. So Bet Freeman packed her satchel, took her baby in her arms, and walked four miles to the village of Sheffield. Once there, she sought out the home of Theodore Sedgwick.

Sedgwick was a compassionate man. He patiently listened as

Bet asked him about the paper in the Ashley study and if it could make her free. He told her he was not sure if the law would apply to her. At that point, Bet said she had overheard them reading the paper in the study and it had said, "all men are born free and equal." And she reminded Sedgwick that when those words were spoken it was he who had responded: "Good! The supreme law of Massachusetts."

Moved by her argument, Sedgwick promised Bet he would look into the matter. Meanwhile, she must return to the Ashley household. When Colonel Ashley arrived to retrieve her, he reprimanded Bet and explained once more that the law did not apply to slaves.

By then, Sedgwick was beginning to wonder if Bet Freeman might be right. The wording in the new Massachusetts Constitution was clear. Should the words *all men* and *free and equal* apply to slaves? Were they legally binding? The questions gnawed at his conscience. Finally, he made an agonizing decision. He prepared a lawsuit on behalf of Elizabeth Freeman against his old friend, John Ashley. He filed the case in the Court of Common Pleas at Great Barrington, Massachusetts.

The case went to trial in August of 1781. Ashley, backed by other concerned slave owners, had hired the best lawyers in the state to refute the legal arguments put forth by Sedgwick.

The jury heard the case, weighed the evidence, and came back with its verdict. According to the new Massachusetts Constitution, John Ashley did not have the right to hold Elizabeth Freeman in servitude for life. She was ordered set free. In addition, she was awarded thirty shillings in silver for damages and five pounds, fourteen shillings, and four pence for costs.

In 1783 Massachusetts became the first state to abolish slavery, the decision based on the wording of the Massachusetts Constitution and the outcome of the *Freeman* case. Connecticut and Rhode Island soon followed suit and, one by one, other New England states outlawed slavery.

Elizabeth Freeman had opened the freedom floodgates for thousands of enslaved African-Americans, but millions more would remain in bondage for generations to come. It would be another 84 years before ratification of the Thirteenth Amendment of the U.S. Constitution legally ended slavery, and another 101 years after that before passage of the 1964 Civil Rights Act finally guaranteed the freedom that Bet Freeman sought when she walked toward the village of Sheffield carrying her child and her satchel.

Jacob de Cardova was not an imposing man in stature or manner. Frail in appearance and soft-spoken, he certainly did not resemble the type of man one associates with a hero of the American West. But no one contributed more to the opening of America's vast Southwest than de Cardova. A dreamer himself, he sold the western adventure to a generation of restless Americans and sparked a mighty migration that carried civilization to a raw land. Yet, he was not an American.

The son of well-to-do Jewish parents, de Cardova was born in Jamaica. As a young man, he founded a newspaper there named the *Kingston Daily Gleaner* and enjoyed success as a publisher. Sickly from childhood, de Cardova was devastated to learn he had tuberculosis. A doctor urged him to leave Jamaica's damp climate for a drier atmosphere.

He emigrated to Philadelphia in the 1830s, not for its climate but because the city had a large and thriving Jewish community. He went to work as a printer, and for a time his health seemed to improve, prompting him to return to Jamaica and attempt to resume his journalistic career. But his health failed him once more.

This time, de Cardova decided he would not return to Philadelphia. The harsh winters there were hardly conducive to an improvement in his condition. He became fascinated to the point of obsession with a place called Texas.

De Cardova had read extensively about Texas and was angered to learn that the Mexican government forbid practice of the Jewish faith. Jews in Texas, he had learned, were forced to give up their faith and swear allegiance to the Catholic Church. If they refused, their property would be confiscated by the state and they would be exiled. When American immigrants in Texas rebelled and began fighting a war for independence from Mexico, de Cardova religiously followed reports of the conflict. The Texas rebels became his heroes. He read their Declaration of Independence and was impressed by its promise of religious freedom. When Sam Houston and his Texans defeated Santa Anna, de Cardova was elated. This, he decided, was where he wanted to be—in Texas, among those hardy men of strong conviction who had struggled against great odds and won their independence.

De Cardova was twenty-nine years old when he stepped onto the docks at Galveston, Texas, to begin a new life. He made his way to Houston, some 30 miles inland, and became a merchant. Just as his business began to turn a profit, his health began to fail him once more. A physician told him he must move from the humid coastal region to a drier climate or risk losing his life. When de Cardova replied that he did not want to leave Texas, the doctor suggested that he consider moving to the wilderness area beyond the Brazos River.

De Cardova turned over his Houston business to his wife and set out westward on horseback. He was awed by the beauty of the land and began to explore its valleys and the rivers that ran through them. Since few maps of the area existed, he made his own. He became an expert on the region, acquiring knowledge of its connecting streams and the quality of its soils. He began purchasing tracts of land and applied for land grants.

By 1845, when the Republic of Texas became the twenty-eighth state of the United States, de Cardova's holdings could be measured in miles more readily than acres. It was a time when Texas's western frontier was still inhabited by ruffians, adventurers, and outlaws, but de Cardova envisioned lush farms in the fertile valleys and cities on the banks of the rivers.

He opened a land and emigration office and became a one-man publicity agency for the region. He traveled extensively outside the state to drum up interest in the Texas frontier. In 1847 he ran for the state legislature on a platform that advocated bringing more people to Texas. Once elected, he fought for laws that would encourage development and reserve certain lands for public use. To publicize his beloved Texas, de Cardova relied on his journalistic background to found a magazine named the *Texas Herald*. It circulated throughout the country, appearing on the counters of crossroads stores, stage stops, trading posts, and railroad depots.

The settlers came—thousands of them—from the Midwest and New England, from the docks of New York and New Orleans, seeking the new beginning promised to them in the *Texas Herald*.

That's
Not
in My
American
History
Book

De Cardova invested every cent he had in land. He resold it to families, often on credit, and often for whatever the individual could pay. He donated lands for public buildings. Remembering his anger upon reading about religious intolerance in Texas under Mexico, he set aside lands for places of worship without regard to faith or denomination. As the region filled with people during the decade of the 1850s, de Cardova prospered. But his vision would become a nightmare.

With the beginning of the Civil War in 1861, everything changed. The war devastated the Texas economy as Union gunboats blockaded the ports of Houston, Galveston, and Indianola, and the flood of new immigrants ceased. The port at Brownsville remained open for a time before being blockaded, but it was a world away from the land of the Brazos. No railroads connected the two, and there were few roads of any kind. Cotton was the cash crop of the Brazos, but the farmers could no longer ship their bales to the lucrative markets back East or to Europe.

Mortgages came due and went unpaid. As the crisis deepened, de Cardova made a decision that would set him apart from other businessmen. He could have saved his own investments by foreclosing on the many small farmers and merchants who owed him money, but his conscience would not allow him to do that. He was the one who had encouraged the settlers to come west on his promise of a new life, and he was determined not to fail them.

Even as de Cardova's creditors threatened him with financial ruin, he sent letters to those who owed him money, informing them that he understood their circumstances and assuring them he would not expect payments on their loans until after the war. His own creditors were not so understanding. They seized his holdings. He was ruined financially, but through it all, he did not foreclose on a single mortgage. With the end of the war, his creditors claimed moneys received from his debtors.

By then, de Cardova was in his late fifties and his health was beginning to fail him once more. He moved into a house on a tract of land on the outskirts of Waco, Texas. The man who had literally given away thousands of acres of land died there in 1868 at age fifty-nine. His house and a few acres surrounding it were all he had left.

But Jacob de Cardova did not die in despair. Across the way was the growing town of Waco. In the valleys around him, farmers were plowing their fields and the weekly toll of church bells echoing over the hills was like medicine to his tired body. The wilderness he had mapped was alive.

Today this prosperous area of the nation is still inhabited by an industrious people, many of them living on land that once belonged to a frail little man from Jamaica. Although some might know his name from local lore, few know the full story of Jacob de Cardova's contribution to Texas and the people beyond the Brazos.

PART
TWO
*The
Midnight
Ride of
Sibyl
Ludington*

In the early 1950s, a plague clouded the American landscape. A mysterious virus stalked the nation's youth like a silent, invisible killer. For generations, it had been devouring young lives. But in the previous three decades the number of its victims had increased dramatically. Those it did not kill, it left hopelessly paralyzed and deformed.

Newspaper artists sometimes depicted the disease as a dragon. Its common name was infantile paralysis, or poliomyelitis, or simply polio.

Polio struck every summer, turning strong bodies into crumpled ones, leaving in its wake withered limbs in steel braces and straps. It was simply expected when the children returned to school each fall that a friend or classmate would have been lost to polio over the summer. Everyone knew a victim—if not in their own family, it was the boy down the street or one on the next street. By the early 1950s, some 50,000 cases per year were being reported, and 1952 alone saw 59,000 new cases.

But in April of 1955 a miracle occurred. It came in the form of an announcement that a vaccine had been discovered that could actually prevent polio. With completion of a series of research field tests, the news media hailed it as the most dramatic breakthrough in the history of medical research.

The hero of the day, the man who slew the polio dragon, was a shy young doctor named Jonas Salk. Stories of his heroic effort to perfect his vaccine filled the newspapers.

In the months prior to final development of the vaccine, Salk had pushed himself to the limits of human endurance. Realizing he was close to a breakthrough, he worked seven days a week, often up to 20 or 30 hours at a time without sleep. He often skipped meals. The public lionized him for his efforts. But that was not the case among those in the scientific community. Behind the scenes, unknown to the public, Salk was being vilified by his peers. At one point some leading scientists even tried to stop distribution of his life-saving vaccine.

Salk's fellow scientists in biological research considered him an outsider, intruding into their domain. In fact, in order to acquire funds for his research, Salk had to go outside normal channels. When he did so, scientists accused him of being a publicity hound. The research establishment was especially jealous of Salk's relationship with Basil O'Connor, the man who supplied much of his funding. As president of the National Foundation for Infantile Paralysis, O'Connor held the purse strings to millions in research dollars. And he believed in Salk.

Basil O'Connor knew firsthand the devastating effects of the disease. His daughter had been stricken with polio. And when O'Connor was a young man, Franklin Roosevelt had been his best friend and law partner, long before becoming president of the United States. O'Connor had seen polio turn an athletic young Roosevelt into a man unable to stand without leg braces and walking sticks. In Jonas Salk, O'Connor found someone who shared his outright hatred for the disease.

Viewed in retrospect, one might understand the opposition of biological research scientists to Salk's methods. He made many transgressions against traditional research. For one thing, the very efficacy of his vaccine toppled one of the most universally accepted (though erroneous) tenets of orthodox virology—the notion that an active virus could not be checked by its own dead viral bodies. That was precisely the path Salk chose to develop his vaccine.

For decades, traditional biologists had been waging what they considered a deliberate, correct, gentleman's fight against polio with efforts focused on treatment rather than prevention. By contrast, Salk fought the dragon like a man possessed, seeking a final cure. He had grown up on the fringes of poverty and developed an attitude more humanist than scientific, a man unwilling to abide senseless rules in the face of a crisis. He flailed against the disease like a punch-drunk street fighter—and he landed a knockout blow.

Finally, his success proved the greatest transgression of all against his fellow scientists. By the 1950s, researching polio was a very big business, and overnight, Salk made further efforts redundant. It was unheard of that an outsider, working independently, could accomplish what the nation's top scientists with their great

That's
Not
in My
American
History
Book

laboratories and countless millions of dollars could not. They expressed their bitterness in rather petty ways, even refusing to accept Salk into the National Academy of Science. The reason? Salk, they contended, was not really a scientist—only a technician.

The public never knew the depths of his colleagues' resentment. It was almost a decade after his discovery before Salk himself would even discuss it. "The worst tragedy that could have befallen me was my success," he told an interviewer. "I knew right away that I was through, that I would be cast out."

But he was not through.

With the polio dragon defeated, he launched a campaign to raise funds to construct the Salk Institute for Biological Studies at Torrey Pines, California. He worked there, surrounded by bright, young scientists until his death at age eighty. Salk later became obsessed with finding a cure for the human immunodeficiency virus (HIV) that causes AIDS. Almost until the day he died, he was trying to catch lightning in a test tube one last time. Perhaps a man is allotted only one miracle in his lifetime.

Today, research scientists work in the laboratories Jonas Salk built, searching for new weapons in the fight against dragons that defy destruction: cancer, AIDS, Alzheimer's, cerebral palsy, multiple sclerosis, and Parkinson's.

Among those scientists at Torrey Pines, waging gentlemanly wars against the microscopic enemies of man, perhaps a new maverick will emerge—a stubborn street fighter who will defeat the odds and capture the lightning that eluded Jonas Salk.

PART THREE

Scandals and Scoundrels

The Underside of History

Were General Custer's soldiers suffering hangovers that fateful morning at Little Big Horn? What made John Quincy Adams accuse Andrew Jackson of murder? Which one of our presidential first ladies turned out to be a shameless thief? Rumor and scandal have always lurked in the shadows of recorded history. But until the last half of the twentieth century, historians traditionally avoided the unsavory side of our nation's past. Some even felt it their duty to provide us with a positive history.

A new attitude, brought on by the evolution of television news and fueled by cynicism over the Warren Commission Report, emerged in the 1960s. Since then, the glare of TV lights has illuminated the deceptions of Vietnam, Watergate, Contragate, Filegate, Monicagate, and others. It leads one to wonder what might have been if those lights were present in past centuries. From that perspective, we will dredge up some of those old scandals and scoundrels from our past and try to separate fact from rumor.

General Misconduct
America's Most Infamous Officer

The most embarrassing defeat ever suffered by the United States military did not take place at Little Big Horn. In happened in 1813 at Lacolle Mill, Canada. That is where 200 British regulars turned back an invasion force of 4,000 Americans. It was the most ignoble defeat in U.S. military history. The reason for the debacle at Lacolle Mill was Gen. James Wilkinson.

In addition to his incompetence as a military officer, Wilkinson was a scoundrel without peer—so unsavory a character, his name has been literally stricken from our history books.

At the outbreak of the war with Great Britain in 1812, Wilkinson was the senior ranking officer in the U.S. military. He was also a con man and thief, manipulating Army supply contracts and pocketing huge sums in the form of kickbacks. He also was a land speculator who duped investors. During the American Revolution, he betrayed George Washington by conspiring with Thomas Conway and Horatio Gates to have Washington removed as commander of the Continental Army. He later conspired with Aaron Burr in a plan to seize New Orleans, conquer Texas, and form a new nation west of the Mississippi River. He then betrayed Burr. He plotted with the governor of Louisiana to jail the governor's political enemies, then turned on him, taking over his territory and terrorizing the citizens of New Orleans. He became a secret agent and spy for the Spanish government, receiving $2,000 a year for his clandestine services, right up until he double-crossed Spain.

Although he was most proficient as a con man, Wilkinson was totally incompetent as a military leader. Regretfully, this shortcoming did not manifest itself until the shooting started in the War of 1812. Wilkinson was somewhat typical of the politically connected appointees occupying positions of responsibility in the U.S. military at the outbreak of the war. Congress would pay dearly for some of those appointments.

★

That's
Not
in My
American
History
Book

Wilkinson was placed in command of American forces on the Canadian border with instructions to invade Canada and capture Montreal. Instead, when confronted by British regulars at Lacolle Mill, he retreated. His cowardly act would result in the British crossing the border to occupy Detroit and burn Buffalo, New York. The result of Wilkinson's incompetence was brought directly home to the Congress in August of 1814, when British troops landed on the shores of Maryland, marched on Washington, D.C., and burned the capital. Finally, it was local militias, not the U.S. Army, that prevailed against the British.

Although his name has been virtually purged from history, Wilkinson's involvement in the Aaron Burr conspiracy made it impossible for historians to completely ignore him.

In 1804, Burr, then vice president of the United States, shot and mortally wounded political adversary Alexander Hamilton in a pistol duel. Although acquitted of any crime, Burr was discredited in Washington. Convinced he had been cheated out of the presidency by Hamilton and Thomas Jefferson, he came up with a plan to seize New Orleans from the United States and use it as a base to invade Texas and create his own nation.

Early in 1805, Burr went to St. Louis to plot with his old friend, General Wilkinson, then commander of all U.S. forces in the Mississippi River Valley. They agreed that Burr would return east to raise money, secure arms, and put together an army. He then would march south to join forces with Wilkinson at Natchez, Mississippi, and their combined armies would occupy New Orleans. Ironically, even as Wilkinson was conspiring to invade Spanish territory, he was being paid to spy for the Spanish government.

By the fall of 1806, Burr had obtained sufficient funding from the British to put together a navy and raise a rebel army. He informed Wilkinson in a coded message that he would be leaving Philadelphia on August 1, 1806 and proceed down the Ohio River Valley gathering men, supplies, and boats along the way. He planned to join forces with Wilkinson at Natchez in December before marching on New Orleans.

By that time, rumors were circulating in Washington that Burr was up to no good. Wilkinson, seeing the proverbial handwriting on the wall, decided to betray his co-conspirator. On October 21, 1806, he sent a message to President Jefferson revealing the details of Burr's plan. Instead of firing Wilkinson, Jefferson inexplicably ordered him to proceed to New Orleans to defend the city against Burr.

Wilkinson went to New Orleans, but instead of defending the city, he took it over. He declared martial law and began firing city officials even as his troops looted homes and businesses. On the pretense he was purging the city of Burr conspirators, he ordered the arrest of anyone who opposed him. The governor of Louisiana, recognizing an opportunity, quickly threw in with Wilkinson to rid New Orleans of his political enemies. It soon became apparent to the governor that his friend the general was arresting his own supporters as well as his enemies.

As property was seized and innocent citizens were thrown into jail, a flurry of lawsuits were filed against Wilkinson and the U.S.

⭐

PART
THREE
*Scandals
and
Scoundrels*

101

An officer and a scoundrel
Gen. James Wilkinson found his true calling in conspiracy and duplicity.
Independence National Historical Park

government. The general reacted by jailing the plaintiffs along with the judges who dared accept their cases.

Meanwhile, Burr's plan was exposed and he was having difficulty raising an army. He was arrested before he could reach Natchez. Although Wilkinson had deceived Burr, the governor, the Spanish, and the politicians in Washington, he did not fool his fellow generals. Gen. Andrew Jackson warned officials in Washington that Wilkinson could not be trusted and sent the following message to Governor William C. C. Claiborne in Louisiana:

That's
Not
in My
American
History
Book

"Be upon the alert. Keep a watchful eye on our general. . . . I fear there is something rotten in Denmark." Unfortunately, the governor did not heed Jackson's advice.

Meanwhile, Gen. Crowles Mead would inform President Jefferson: "It is believed here that General Wilkinson is the soul of the conspiracy."

Why Jefferson allowed Wilkinson to retain his command is one of the unexplained mysteries of our past. The fact that Wilkinson had powerful supporters in Congress is the most likely answer. In spite of his involvement with Burr and his behavior in New Orleans, he continued to be promoted until, by 1812, he was the senior officer in the United States Army. It was only after the disaster at Lacolle Mill, when his incompetence as a military commander became apparent to all, that he finally was relieved of command.

In 1814, Wilkinson was quietly hauled before a court martial hearing. Despite a mountain of evidence detailing his corrupt dealings, treasonous alliance with Spain, and illegal behavior in New Orleans, he was quickly acquitted and given an honorable discharge. It has been speculated that the acquittal was a tradeoff to protect the careers of certain fellow officers, some high-ranking government officials, and perhaps a congressman or two involved in Wilkinson's schemes. Following his trial, Wilkinson retired to Mexico, where he lived very well on an ill-gained fortune.

My Dishonorable Opponent

Politics and political mudslinging have been around almost from the day prehistoric man discovered mud. However, over the past two centuries American politicians have managed to refine the art—sometimes elevating it to creative heights, but more often dragging it to bottomless lows.

In the creative category, one of the strangest campaigns ever waged was the one by George Smathers against Claude Pepper for the U.S. Senate in Florida in 1950. In his campaign speeches, Smathers began referring to Pepper as "a known extrovert." He spat out the words with such disdain, many in his audiences assumed the worst of Pepper. While Pepper was trying to figure out how to respond, Smathers revealed that his opponent's sister was "a thespian." He then accused Pepper's brother of being "a practicing homo sapiens." He charged that while attending college, Pepper "matriculated on campus," and that he "engaged in celibacy" before he was married.

Smathers won the election.

If that was the high point of political creativity, the low had to take place in Louisiana in 1932, when Earl Long called a political enemy "A big-bellied, lily-livered liar and the crookedest man who ever lived." The reference was to his brother, Huey Long. On another occasion, Earl became so enraged at his brother he called him a son of a bitch before fully analyzing the implication.

A favorite Earl Long tactic was to follow an opponent around and inspire impromptu debate by heckling from the audience. Not only did it save money, it allowed Earl to control the agenda for discussion. However, on one occasion the practice backfired. Huey, then seeking election as a U.S. senator, was telling a large crowd what he had done for the people of Louisiana when Earl's shrill voice came from the crowd.

"I know one person you ain't done nothin' for—your brother!"

That's
Not
in My
American
History
Book

104

"I've done something for you, Earl," Huey replied. "I built a big mental hospital down at Jackson and I had them reserve a room for you."

Later, when Huey ran away to avoid a fistfight with Earl, he explained his cowardly action to reporters, "I ain't gonna fight Earl 'cause he bites." In fact, Earl had perfected ear biting as a means of dealing with adversaries, long before anyone had heard of Mike Tyson. He was arrested in New Orleans after engaging in a fight with a political opponent who complained to police that "Earl Long ran across the street, punched me in the face and bit my ear."

The Long brothers later patched up their differences and became political allies. Earl was a three-time governor of Louisiana, and Huey was a U.S. senator and presidential contender when he was assassinated in 1935.

The Longs were not the only brother duo to have differences. Jimmy Carter's worst enemy was his beer-swilling brother, Billy, whose drunken antics were a continuing source of embarrassment to the president. The final straw was when Billy relieved himself on an airport runway in front of the Washington press corps. Jimmy sent him home to Plains, Georgia, with instructions not to come back.

Physical violence in politics did not originate with the Long brothers. Back in 1798, a scandalous incident took place in the U.S. Congress when Representative Roger Griswold of Connecticut made disparaging remarks about the war record of Representative Matthew Lyon of Vermont. Lyon reacted by spitting on Griswold. That provoked Griswold to strike Lyon repeatedly with his walking stick. (Unfortunately, all of this took place before C-Span.) In addition to the physical pain and indignity that resulted from being caned, Lyon was convicted of sedition, fined $1,000, and spent four months in jail.

Yet another infamous caning incident took place in 1856, at the height of the debate on slavery, when Representative Preston Brooks of South Carolina took exception to remarks about his family made by Senator Charles Sumner of Massachusetts. Brooks was so enraged, he walked into the Senate chamber and attacked Sumner with his walking cane. Brooks later expressed regret over the incident, noting that it had cost him a perfectly good walking stick, although he had managed to salvage the gold-plated handle.

Theodore Roosevelt did not need a cane to contend with political adversaries. In 1883, when he was a member of the New York

Assembly, he decked a Democratic opponent with one punch. When the man got up, Roosevelt knocked him down again. The man's offense: He had made fun of Roosevelt's clothes.

Roosevelt also participated in one of the most violent presidential nominating conventions in the nation's history. It took place in 1912 at Chicago when Roosevelt, a former president, challenged incumbent William Howard Taft for the Republican nomination. There were riots and fistfights inside and outside the convention hall. Barbed wire had to be placed around the podium to protect speakers from the delegates. It would be sixty years before another convention could match it for riotous behavior. That one took place in 1972 at (where else?) Chicago.

Going back in time, the struggle to fill the leadership void left by George Washington's departure from the presidency resulted in some bitter political battles between founding fathers John Adams, Alexander Hamilton, and Thomas Jefferson. The same Jefferson who had so eloquently penned the Declaration of Independence lowered his standards to write of Hamilton, "[He is] hotheaded, all imagination and no judgment . . . disrespectful and even indecent." A Philadelphia newspaper editor who supported Jefferson wrote of President Adams, "He is blind, bald, toothless and querulous." Considering that there was nothing wrong with Adams's eyesight, the description was only seventy-five percent correct.

In 1804 the deadliest of all political confrontations took place. That is when Vice President Aaron Burr shot and mortally wounded Alexander Hamilton in a pistol duel after Hamilton conspired to deny Burr the presidency. Attempts to prosecute Burr failed. Having lost the presidency to Jefferson, Burr attempted to seize Louisiana and establish his own nation west of the Mississippi, but the venture failed. Burr eventually failed at just about everything, with one notable exception: He enjoyed incredible success as an aging Romeo. He fathered at least two illegitimate children when he was in his seventies. When he was eighty years old, Burr's second wife sued him for divorce on the grounds of adultery.

Another famous pistol duel took place when congressmen John Randolph of Virginia and Henry Clay of Kentucky met on the field of honor. Clay fired his pistol into the air even as Randolph shot a hole through Clay's coat. Brought to his senses by the near tragedy, Randolph apologized for spoiling a perfectly good gar-

That's
Not
in My
American
History
Book

ment. Although it might have proven effective, the political pistol duel never quite caught on as a substitute for term limits.

Perhaps the dirtiest of all presidential campaigns took place in 1828 when Andrew Jackson ran against incumbent John Quincy Adams. Jackson's political opponents portrayed him as a blood-thirsty military tyrant, a drunkard, gambler, womanizer, and even a murderer. His wife, Rachel, was dragged into the campaign and her name besmirched when she and Jackson were accused of living together in an invalid marriage because she was not legally divorced from her first husband. An Adams pamphlet asked the question: "Ought a convicted adulteress and her paramour husband be placed in the highest office of this free and Christian land?" The murder accusation stemmed from Jackson's execution of several army deserters in the War of 1812.

Political discourse in the Senate, 1856 Representative Preston Brooks attacks Senator Charles Sumner. *New York Public Library*

Jackson supporters responded by accusing Adams of living in sin with his wife before they were married. Adams also was accused of supplying a beautiful American virgin for the sexual amusement of the czar of Russia and with using public funds to purchase "gambling devices" for his own entertainment in the White House. The "devices" turned out to be a pool table and chess set. When Jackson won the election, so deep was the animosity that Adams refused to attend the inauguration.

Jackson was plagued throughout his presidency by charges of past infidelities. A scandal referred to as the "Petticoat War" threatened to topple his administration. It began on January 1, 1829 when Jackson's friend, John Eaton, married a beautiful young widow from Tennessee named Peggy O'Neal Timberlake. Peggy, a barmaid and dancer, earlier was linked romantically with Jackson. There was speculation Jackson had encouraged Eaton to marry her to remove pressure from himself. When Jackson named Eaton to his cabinet, the socially elite ladies of Washington, some of them wives of cabinet members, threw a collective fit. They spread wild rumors about Peggy and Jackson and demanded Eaton's resignation. Their husbands were drawn into the conflict

**PART
THREE**
*Scandals
and
Scoundrels*

107

Poor loser Aaron Burr shoots Alexander Hamilton in a duel. Burr blamed Hamilton for cheating him out of the presidency.

and by the time the Petticoat War concluded, Jackson's cabinet had resigned, along with Vice President John C. Calhoun who, incidentally, Jackson once threatened to hang.

Any number of other politicians overcame sexual scandals to occupy the White House. Well before Bill Clinton's questionable behavior with Gennifer Flowers, Paula Jones, Monica Lewinski,

That's
Not
in My
American
History
Book

108

Kathleen Willey, Dolly Browning, Juanita Broaddrick, and others, there was President Franklin Pierce. He was a notorious alcoholic and womanizer. His drinking became such a problem that he once had to resign from the U.S. Senate; but that did not prevent him from running for the presidency in 1850. Even more remarkable than his entry into the race was the fact that he won.

President Warren Harding's broom-closet trysts with Carrie Phillips were common knowledge around the nation's capital, if not among the electorate. Less well known was that he fathered a child with another mistress and was accused of attempting to seduce young girls.

James Buchanan, the bachelor president, overcame questions concerning his sexual orientation to win the presidential election of 1856. For many years he shared a home with William Rufus de Vane King, who was openly homosexual. King, who eventually became vice president in the Pierce administration, was nicknamed "Miss Nancy" by his Washington colleagues. In spite of his relationship with King, Buchanan constantly was pursued by female admirers and even came close to getting married a time or two. The question of his sexual leanings was frequently whispered but never resolved.

Election fraud has been with us as long as there have been elections. In 1876, the Republican Party managed to blatantly steal a presidential election and put Rutherford B. Hayes in the White House. Democrat Samuel B. Tilden won the popular vote and the electoral vote; but Republicans managed to challenge the results and maneuver the election into the House of Representatives, where they held a majority. But it was a Democrat who tipped the balance in Hayes's favor. Representative Francis T. Nichols broke a deadlock when he cast Louisiana's electoral votes for Hayes. He did so in exchange for a Republican promise to remove occupying federal troops from his state.

On the other side of the political spectrum, the Democrats were accused of stealing the 1960 election when Republicans charged that Chicago Mayor Richard Daley manipulated the Illinois election returns and put John F. Kennedy in the White House.

In the election of 1884, presidential candidate Grover Cleveland became a target for flying political mud. Supporters of James G. Blaine charged that Cleveland had fathered a child out of wedlock. The mother was Marie Crofts Halpin, an attractive and somewhat controversial widow who had a reputation for dating married politicians around Washington, D.C. Blaine backers paraded in the streets, chanting "Ma, Ma, where's my Pa?"

Instead of denying the charge, Cleveland admitted he was the father; his forthrightness helped him win the election. In answer to the taunting of his opponents, Cleveland backers responded, "Gone to the White House, haw, haw, haw!"

Ironically, later there was supposition that Cleveland might not have been the child's father after all, and that the president had been protecting marriages of his friends who were among Marie Halpin's many paramours.

Hubert Humphrey faced an entirely different situation when he ran for president in 1968. He was bombarded by rumors that had no element of truth at all. One rumor being circulated was

★

PART
THREE
*Scandals
and
Scoundrels*

109

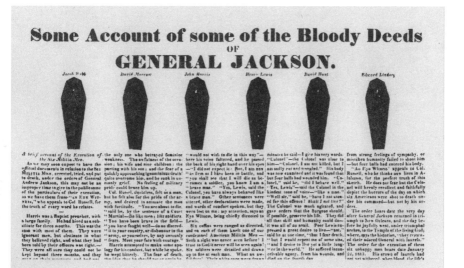

Our forefathers' mudslinging Andrew Jackson is accused of being a murderer in John Quincy Adams's campaign literature. *Granger Collection*

that, when stopped by the police, not only was Humphrey drunk, but he had a "well-known call girl" in the car with him. Humphrey would not lower himself to respond to the charge and lost the election.

Other politicians were undone by an inability or unwillingness to refute another political sin: Communism. From World War I until the 1950s, "red baiting" became a familiar campaign tactic. In 1932, Robert Reynolds won a U.S. Senate seat by painting his

★

That's
Not
in My
American
History
Book

110

opponent, Cameron Morrison, with a "red" brush. As Reynolds stumped through North Carolina, he carried with him a small jar of Russian caviar. At each campaign stop, he would hold the little jar aloft and proclaim: "Cam eats Red Russian fish eggs that cost two dollars a jar." Reynolds then would assure the crowd that good old North Carolina hen eggs were good enough for him.

In 1950, opponents of U.S. Senator Millard Tydings accused the Maryland Democrat of being soft on Communism. They doctored a photograph showing Tydings with American Communist Party leader Earl Browder. Although Tydings had never met Browder, the controversy created by the fake photograph caused him to retire from public life after twenty-four years in the Senate.

In 1934, one of California's dirtiest elections took place when gubernatorial candidate Upton Sinclair was accused of being a

The Petticoat War Peggy O'Neal Timberlake is shown dancing for the president and his cabinet. The performance never took place.

Communist and an advocate of "free love." He might have overcome those charges, but could not survive accusations that he was "against the Boy Scouts."

Beyond doubt the most unusual election in U.S. history took place in Texas in 1948, when Lyndon B. Johnson ran against Coke Stevenson for the U.S. Senate. According to election records, several hundred deceased persons at Alice, Texas, managed to escape their graves, march to the polls, and vote for Johnson before returning to their places of rest. At one precinct, some 200 graveyard residents not only voted, they apparently managed to line up alphabetically in order to do so. Johnson won the election by 87 votes.

At least one other future president went to Washington in an election tainted by fraud. In 1934, the infamous "Pendergast Machine" in Kansas City, Missouri, helped send Harry S. Truman to the U.S. Senate with the assistance of some 50,000 fraudulent votes added to the statewide registration rolls.

There was nothing subtle about the dirty politics engaged in by the Pendergast Machine. When all else failed and Thomas Pendergast's slate of candidates for city offices appeared doomed in 1934, the Kansas City strongman hired a group of thugs and armed them with machine guns and shotguns. Riding in black limousines with no license plates, they shot up the opposing party's headquarters, beat scores of poll watchers, and chased voters away from polling places. When the election day mayhem was over, four people were dead and eleven hospitalized. Ten of Pendergast's twelve candidates won, and Harry Truman rode the Pendergast "landslide" all the way to Washington, D.C., as Missouri's new senator.

Political campaigns frequently employ scare tactics. In 1964, Democrats accused Republican presidential candidate Barry Goldwater of being a warmonger. They also found a quack psychiatrist who questioned Goldwater's sanity. They then reinforced the image of a madman with his finger on the atomic button by airing a television commercial showing a little girl picking flowers on a hillside just before being blown up by a nuclear bomb. Democrat Lyndon Johnson, the peace candidate who authorized the commercial, promised voters he would never send American boys to fight a war that Asian boys should be fighting. Johnson won the election and promptly expanded the war, eventually deploying 500,000 troops in Vietnam. The war ultimately claimed the lives of more than 58,000 American soldiers.

Finally, there was CREEP and the infamous presidential election of 1972. CREEP, which stood for the Committee to Re-Elect the President, devised a "dirty tricks campaign" designed to keep Republican Richard Nixon in the White House. Instead of beating people with rifle butts or showing little girls being blown up on television, CREEP planted phony letters and memos and spread

That's
Not
in My
American
History
Book

untrue rumors in a campaign of deliberate misinformation against Democratic candidates. They created phony organizations with radical agendas and linked them to Democrats. They chased Senator Henry Jackson from the race by starting the somewhat paradoxical rumor that he was a homosexual who fathered a child out of wedlock. Their personal attacks on front-running Democrat Edmund Muskie and his wife caused Muskie to break into tears during a press conference, eliminating him as a candidate because presidents are not supposed to cry. And, of course, there was the famous rumor of a drunken Hubert Humphrey riding around with a call girl.

CREEP's dirty tricks would culminate with a break-in at the Democratic headquarters at the Watergate Hotel in Washington, D.C. The ensuing scandal resulted in Richard Nixon becoming the only president to resign from office while reinforcing the old adage that he who slings mud is likely to get some on himself.

Don't ask, don't tell
Bachelor president James Buchanan lived with a homosexual but dated some of Washington's most beautiful women.
New-York Historical Society

Beyond the Call of Duty
Military Sex Scandals

The tar brush of scandal is not reserved exclusively for politicians. The reputations of some of our greatest military heroes have been stained by it.

America's three most popular generals during World War II had their names sullied by sex scandals at one time or another during their military careers. Fortunate for the war effort, they survived and today are revered as American icons. The three were Dwight Eisenhower, George Patton, and Douglas MacArthur.

Although it was not widely reported until after the war, most journalists were aware that General Eisenhower was having an affair with his attractive chauffeur, Kay Summersby, even as he attended to his duties as supreme commander of the Allied Forces in Europe. By the end of the war, his reputation as a military hero so far overshadowed rumors of his infidelities that he was twice elected president of the United States, allowing him to turn his attention to other interests, like golf.

Gen. George Patton's reputation for bizarre behavior began not on the battlefield, but in the bedroom. While stationed in Hawaii before World War II, he allegedly had an affair with his young niece. Although the incident resulted in an estrangement from his family, it did not interfere with his military career. As commander of the Third Army in World War II, he became a national hero.

Assigned to a command in the Philippines, Douglas MacArthur was sailing to Manila when he became enamored with a fellow passenger, a young lady half his age. He talked her into moving in with him, and the two happily resided in luxury in a Manila hotel suite for several years. In 1930, when MacArthur was named U.S. Army chief of staff and called back to Washington, D.C., his lover accompanied him. Unfortunately for MacArthur, she talked freely about their relationship, and her indiscretion led

⭐

That's
Not
in My
American
History
Book

114

to arguments. MacArthur reportedly paid her $15,000 to keep quiet. Supposedly, he was more concerned about his mother finding out about the affair than his friends in Washington.

Perhaps Eisenhower, Patton, and MacArthur felt comfortable in their relationships because their commander in chief was having an affair of his own. Franklin Roosevelt had a continuing relationship with Lucy Mercer, his wife's social secretary. Although he repeatedly promised his wife he would end the relationship, Lucy was at his bedside when he died at Warm Springs, Georgia, in 1945.

Earlier in our history, several Civil War generals were accompanied by mistresses during their campaigns in the field. The most notorious womanizer of that era might have been Union Gen. Judson Kilpatrick. Not only did his favorite mistress accompany him, she wore a matching uniform and was accused to trying to boss the troops around.

On the Confederate side, Gen. Earl Van Dorn had his hands full trying to outmaneuver Union armies in Tennessee, Arkansas, and Mississippi. But he still found time to have an adulterous affair with the wife of a doctor. The spurned doc responded by shooting Van Dorn in the back and then fleeing behind Union lines, where he was greeted as a hero.

The practice of bringing a mistress along on military cam-

Conduct unbecoming an officer
Generals Dwight Eisenhower and George Patton both had sexual indiscretions but managed to dodge major scandals. *National Archives & Records Administration*

A little R&R
Gen. Douglas MacArthur
kept a live-in lover while
stationed in Manila.
*National Archives & Records
Administration*

paigns might have been inspired by examples set by British generals during the American Revolution. The two most notorious incidents involved generals William Howe and John Burgoyne.

According to reports by his troops, when John Burgoyne brought his army down from Canada to invade upstate New York, he also brought his fun-loving mistress. One soldier wrote that the general spent his nights "singing, drinking, gambling and carousing with his mistress." He should have gotten more rest. At Saratoga, he was outwitted and defeated by Benedict Arnold, who also had a reputation as a ladies' man. Back in Philadelphia, while recuperating from a wound received in the battle, Arnold became involved with a teenage girl who helped influence him to betray his country.

Meanwhile, General Howe, the commander in chief of British forces in America and relentless pursuer of George Washington's Continental Army in the early stages of the war, had his reputation soiled by an affair with the wife of one of his subordinate officers.

The Howe affair became so well known, his troops made up a song about it:

> *Sir William, he, as snug as a flea,*
> *Lay all this time a-snoring,*
> *Nor dreamed of harm as he lay warm,*
> *In bed with Mrs. Loring.*

That's
Not
in My
American
History
Book

Even in the contemporary military, the tradition continues. In 1998 Gen. David Hale, a major general in the U.S. Army, was accused of being involved with the wives of several subordinate officers. Under pressure from the Department of Defense, he retired, even as a scandal broke over the antics of his commander in chief with a young intern in the Oval Office of the White House.

Bolsheviks and Anarchists
Terrorism in the Early Twentieth Century

 A mysterious mad bomber was sending deadly packages through the mails. There was a sinister plot afoot to detonate a massive explosion in a vehicle parked in front of a public building. A mood of intolerance swept the land, and anti-immigration sentiment was on the rise. A fear of terrorism permeated the public consciousness, and the government had declared a war on terrorists. In just one year, the U.S. Congress introduced no less than seventy antiterrorist bills.

The 1990s? No, it was 1919.

If history does not repeat itself, it comes close enough often enough to keep the adage alive. That was illustrated in the 1990s when authorities were frantically searching for an elusive mail bomber, terrorists were hatching a plan to bomb the World Trade Center, and Timothy McVeigh was plotting to blow up a federal office building in Oklahoma City. It was an eerie reenactment of events that took place in 1919, when a similar search was under way for a mysterious mail bomber, and a plot was being hatched to set off a mega-bomb at a landmark building in the heart of New York City.

The earlier reign of terror began on the night of April 25, 1919. Witnesses saw a car pull up to a mail collection box on 28th Street in New York City, and a shadowy figure emerged from the car to carefully place several small packages in the box.

Four days later in Atlanta, Georgia, a maid at the home of U.S. Senator Thomas Hardwick collected the morning mail and placed it on a table in the study. Senator Hardwick, the former chairman of a committee that had recently recommended strict limitations on U.S. immigration, was out of town at the time. Mrs. Hardwick sat at the table that morning and began opening the day's mail.

Among the envelopes, she found a small package. It immedi-

★

That's
Not
in My
American
History
Book

118

ately drew her attention because it had been misaddressed to their previous address at Sandersville, Georgia. The return address was Gimble Brothers, the famous department store in New York City. The word *sample* had been stamped on the package. Because it was about the size of a pencil box, Mrs. Hardwick assumed it contained free pencils. She handed the package to the maid and resumed opening the other mail.

As the maid untied the cord securing the package, there was a blinding explosion. Small bits of metal that had been packed around the explosive flew in all directions, splintering furniture and shattering vases. Both of the maid's hands were blown off. Mrs. Hardwick's upper body was badly burned, and the bodies of both women were riddled with lacerations. Miraculously, both survived.

Investigators from the Department of Justice were amazed that the women were not killed, because they already knew the makeup of the bomb. Just twenty-four hours earlier, a similar "Gimbles" package had arrived on the desk of Mayor Ole Hanson in Seattle, Washington. The mayor recently had denounced terrorist elements who advocated anarchy as he stumped for reelection, and had received several death threats as a result of his statements. Suspicious of receiving any unordered package, Hanson called the police. Government agents were called in and the package was dismantled. It was a carefully crafted bomb.

The authorities were impressed that so much destructive potential could be packed into so small a package. It consisted of a hollowed-out piece of wood measuring three by six inches and about one inch thick. Inside was a homemade stick of dynamite that had been soaked in nitroglycerin. Small pieces of metal were packed around the dynamite. Three percussion caps were attached to a cord that secured the wrapping. It was rigged to explode when the recipient untied the cord.

The Atlanta bombing, and the attempt in Seattle, made headline news across the nation. The day after the Atlanta tragedy, in New York City, a postal employee named Charles Caplan was enjoying his day off and reading his newspaper when the word *Gimbles* caused him to pause. He remembered that several days earlier he had set aside several packages for return to Gimbles because they lacked sufficient postage. The packages were identical in size and appearance to the one described in the news story.

Caplan rushed to the post office. There on a shelf, just as he had left them, were sixteen "Gimbles" packages. His supervisor notified the police, setting off a mad scramble to search every shelf in every postal facility in the nation. A total of thirty-four bombs were found in various postal buildings in the New York area. All had been held up for insufficient postage. Only the two had slipped through.

Even more shocking than the number of bombs were the names and addresses on them. The mailing list read like a *Who's Who* of the nation's business and governmental leaders. Bombs had been addressed to J. P. Morgan and John D. Rockefeller. They were destined for Supreme Court Justice Oliver Wendell Holmes, Judge Kenesaw Mountain Landis, U.S. Attorney General Mitchell Palmer, and Postmaster General Albert Sidney Burleson.

Mitchell Palmer placed blame for the bombs on radical Bolsheviks and publicly vowed to wipe out the "Red menace" that, in his words, was "aiming a dagger at the very heart of America."

To understand Palmer's rhetoric, one must understand the sentiments of the time. Never have the citizens of the United States been more intolerant of foreigners than immediately following World War I. Wartime propaganda had demonized anyone with a German, Italian, or Middle European name. The Bolsheviks had seized control in Russia, and many in America were convinced there was a widespread conspiracy to bring that revolution to the United States. Added to the mix was a small but hard-core group of anarchists determined to disrupt the nation's government and commerce through terrorism.

In 1919 there was no FBI or CIA to contend with such threats. There was only a small Bureau of Investigation in the office of the attorney general. Under Palmer's guidance, it soon became a much larger operation. Palmer sent agents undercover to penetrate every organization that might be considered remotely radical.

Some two months after the Atlanta bombing, Palmer had just left his library and was upstairs preparing to retire for the evening when an explosion went off downstairs. The blast was so strong it blew out the front wall of his house, destroying the library where he had been only minutes before. Windows were shattered several blocks away. When police arrived, they found the mangled remains of the bomber in Palmer's front yard, indicating that the bomb went off prematurely, killing him before he could place it against the house. In his clothing was a copy of *Plain Words*, a radi-

That's
Not
in My
American
History
Book

cal publication produced by an organization whose goal was to overthrow the U.S. government.

Driven by anger, Palmer set in motion what can only be described as a purge. His targets were Russian and Middle European immigrants. Meetings of suspected radical groups were broken up by gun-wielding agents who handcuffed and hauled away those in attendance. Labor union halls were raided and their files ransacked. The raids even extended to private homes and eventually the nation's university campuses, where warrants were obtained to search the files of liberal professors for incriminating correspondence.

More than 6,000 people were arrested across the nation—600 in Boston alone. Almost all of them were innocent of any wrongdoing and were quickly released by the courts. However, hundreds never made it to court. They were simply placed on ships and deported to Europe and Russia as undesirables.

For a time Palmer enjoyed popular support in his crusade to rid the nation of the Red menace. Supporters began touting him for the presidency, and President Woodrow Wilson went so far as to declare that "Mitchell Palmer would make a good president." But Palmer's zeal would lead to his downfall. As the courts continued to release hundreds of the accused and newspapers started reporting horror stories of individual injustice, it became obvious that Palmer was a man out of control. If, indeed, there was a Red menace, the public soon realized it did not include the widespread conspiracy claimed by Palmer. It was apparent the bombings were being carried out by a small corps of radicals dedicated to anarchy.

By the end of the summer of 1920, the Red hysteria had subsided. But the bombers had one final, deadly card to play in their hide-and-seek war with Mitchell Palmer.

The time was noon on September 16, 1920. The place was Wall Street, New York City, directly in front of the J. P. Morgan building, in the very heart of the nation's financial and business community. Executives and office workers were pouring from high rises onto the street for the lunch hour. Some of them later recalled seeing a rather seedy-looking man driving a horse-drawn delivery wagon down the street. He parked the wagon in front of the Morgan building, tethered the horse to a post, and calmly walked away, disappearing into the crowd.

The blast came at 12:05. It was a massive explosion, accompanied by a blinding flash. The concussion sent bodies tumbling like rag dolls. What was described as a great cloud, "like a mushroom," rose high into the air and rained debris back onto the street. Shock waves from the explosion were felt across the river in Brooklyn.

As the smoke and dust settled, the cries of victims could be heard. Dead and injured littered the street. Some were partially naked, their bodies mangled, their clothing having been blown away by the force of the blast. Some of the wounded lay helpless in the street with their clothing on fire. Thirty-five died in the explosion. Scores more were seriously injured.

The inside of the famous House of Morgan looked like a war zone. Glass and debris had been blown through offices. A clerk was found dead at his desk. Others in the building suffered serious wounds.

All buildings in the immediate vicinity were heavily damaged by the explosion. Windows were shattered for blocks in every direction. The wagon that carried the bomb had simply disappeared. The horse that innocently delivered the deadly cargo was blown to bits.

A sweeping investigation was launched, and it was determined the bomb consisted of TNT surrounded by large chunks of metal cut from cast-iron window weights. The only practical physical clues remaining were the shoes of the horse. Detectives managed to locate the blacksmith who had made the shoes, but there the search stalled. The perpetrator was never found.

The explosion that claimed so many innocent lives also proved to be the death knell for the more radical elements among those dedicated to overthrowing the U.S. government with terrorism. Those bent on revolution set up secret societies and cells, went underground, and worked clandestinely in an effort to achieve their goals.

Although the Red menace scare periodically resurfaced during the first half of the twentieth century, it would be more than seven decades before a similar reign of terror was repeated in the United States. And the World Trade Center, a memorial at the federal building in Oklahoma City, and images of Ted Kazenski in a courtroom stand as reminders that history, indeed, repeats itself.

For Lease

The White House

President Bill Clinton was accused of renting out rooms in the White House in exchange for campaign contributions. That was nothing compared to Arthur Furguson's enterprise. He leased the entire building.

Arthur Furguson was a dapper little Scotsman, always immaculate in dress and charming in manner. In 1925 he arrived in Washington, D.C., and visited the White House, Washington Monument, the newly completed Lincoln Memorial, and other national landmarks. But Furguson was not a typical tourist. He was not there to marvel at those great national monuments. He was there to sell them.

Furguson might have been the best salesman who ever lived. He began his illustrious career as just another small-time scam artist working the streets of London, but by the time he arrived in America he was in a category by himself—a con man without peer. The transformation came abruptly one summer when Furguson made a discovery that would change his life, as well as the lives of those with whom he came into contact. He discovered that Americans are gullible.

In that one summer in London, he managed to sell Nelson's Column in Trafalgar Square for $30,000 (he reluctantly agreed to include the lions in the deal); he sold Big Ben for a bargain-basement price of $5,000; and accepted a $10,000 good-faith down payment on the sale of Buckingham Palace.

With Scotland Yard detectives hot on his heels, Furguson boarded a ship bound for America. It was a logical choice of destination, considering that all of his best customers seemed to come from there.

Furguson had been in Washington only briefly when, posing as a government official, he managed to lease the White House to a cattle rancher for ninety-nine years at a cost of $100,000 per year. The first annual payment, of course, was due in advance. How could an otherwise sane individual believe the government would want to lease the White House? Furguson had a convincing explanation. They were going to build an even grander residence for the president closer to the Capitol Building. Furguson convinced the rancher that the income from tours of the old White House would cover the cost of the lease and return a handsome profit. The deal consummated, Furguson quickly caught a train for New York City with a satchel full of money, leaving it to government officials to explain to the rancher that the White House was not available for lease.

⭐
**PART
THREE**
*Scandals
and
Scoundrels*

123

Upon arriving in New York with a nest egg that might have lasted him a lifetime, Furguson decided to go straight. But that was before he saw the Statue of Liberty.

Furguson was admiring the monument like any other tourist when a gentleman from Sydney, Australia, wandered up and commented on its imposing beauty. Temptation overcame resistance. Yes, Furguson agreed, it was a marvelous work; and it was a terrible shame they had to sell it.

When the Aussie expressed surprise that the Statue of Liberty would be for sale, Furguson explained that the ship channel for New York Harbor had to be widened, and the government was left with no choice but to sell the statue and have it relocated. Furguson also expressed regret that, as a high-ranking government official, he was the one assigned the distasteful task of finding a buyer and negotiating a deal.

Furguson kept the con going, growing more nervous with each passing day as the Australian tried to raise the $100,000 deposit from business associates back in Sydney. Furguson was well aware that the longer a scam continues, the greater its chance for failure; but the lure of completing the greatest con of his career inspired him to keep the Australian dangling on the line. His worst fear was realized when the intended victim finally grew suspicious and visited the police. Instead of showing up with a bank note, the Australian arrived with the cops and Furguson was arrested.

Convicted of fraud, he was sentenced to five years in prison. When the time came for his release in 1930, he was hauled back into court. Threatened with the possibility of deportation, Furguson agreed to several conditions before the judge agreed to release him. Among them, he promised authorities he would stop selling

**That's
Not
in My
American
History
Book**

national monuments. To remove him from temptation, Furguson also agreed to leave town. The judge suggested that California might be a nice place for him to live.

Furguson moved to Los Angeles. There he lived out his years in relative luxury from the proceeds of his past scams, augmented by an occasional small-time swindle, just to keep in practice.

But Arthur Furguson never again made the big score—perhaps fearful of returning to a jail cell or maybe humbled by the realization that, in Los Angeles, he was surrounded by experts.

The Rebel Who Refused to Surrender

The U.S. Civil War officially ended in the spring of 1865. But for one Confederate cavalry officer and a small band of followers, the struggle continued until 1869.

The central character in this little-known chapter in American history was an unreconstructed Confederate officer named Robert J. Lee, not to be confused with Robert E. Lee, who was a distant cousin. The event took place in the wilds of North Texas, where Captain Lee held off the United States Army for four bloody years.

Unlike his more famous relative, Captain Lee did not surrender his sword when the war ended. He simply climbed on his horse in Tennessee and rode back home to his father's farm near Pilot Grove, Texas. Captain Lee had served with distinction under legendary Gen. Nathan Bedford Forrest to the bitter end of the war.

Also, unlike most of his fellow Southerners, Lee returned home much as he had left—mounted on a fine-blooded horse, dressed in a splendid uniform, plume waving from his hat band, and sword and gun still at his side. His appearance was in sharp contrast to thousands of former Confederate soldiers in tattered clothing, many without shoes, wearily walking home.

Upon Lee's arrival in Pilot Grove, his appearance and haughty manner upset local Union sympathizers. In the years preceding the war, immigrants from the Midwest who were loyal to the Union had flocked to north Texas. Sentiments were sharply divided in the region. The leader of the Unionists was a Grayson County businessman named Lewis Peacock. He had organized the local Union League and was its president. In that capacity, backed by a group of ruffians turned peace officers and a federal circuit judge, Peacock set out to reap revenge on those Southern sympathizers who had opposed him during the war. Among those he could not intimidate was the inherently arrogant Bob Lee.

★

That's

Not

in My

American

History

Book

While others were careful to avoid confrontation with Peacock and his henchmen, Lee continued to wear his pistol and ride into town on his fine horse to spend what seemed to be an endless supply of twenty-dollar gold pieces. That rankled Peacock because most ex-Confederates did not dare wear a pistol into a town controlled by the Union League, and few had money at all—much less the kind of fortune young Lee seemed to possess.

There was nothing mysterious about the source of Bob Lee's gold coins. His father, Daniel Lee, was a wealthy man when he moved from Virginia to Texas in the late 1830s. Throughout the war there were rumors that, instead of converting his money to Confederate currency, the old man purchased gold coins and buried them in a keg on his farm. Bob Lee's spending habits in town seemed to confirm the rumor.

It was two months after Bob Lee's return when Peacock showed up at the Lee farm, accompanied by a contingent of federal soldiers who promptly surrounded the house. The commander of the troops placed Lee under arrest for alleged war crimes committed during his service in the Confederate Army. Lee was informed that he would be taken to Sherman, some 30 miles distant, where he would be tried.

En route to Sherman, Peacock drew his prisoner aside for a private talk. He informed Lee he could get the charges dropped for a payment of two thousand dollars. Left with little choice, Lee agreed to the terms. He gave Peacock the forty dollars in his pocket and signed a promissory note for the balance. But he had no intention of paying the balance.

Upon being released, Lee went directly to the authorities and filed extortion and kidnapping charges against Peacock. When nothing came of the charges, Lee complained to the commander at the headquarters of the 5th Military District in Austin, causing Peacock embarrassment if not prosecution. Lee's defiance of Peacock and the Union League elevated him to hero status among the area's ex-rebel soldiers, a role that he seemed to enjoy.

Several weeks after the incident, Lee met two Union League members on a street in Pilot Grove and an argument ensued. As he turned to walk away, one of the men drew a pistol and shot him. Friends placed him in a wagon and took him to a doctor who removed the bullet and sent him home to recuperate. Several nights later, the doctor was called to his door in the middle of the night and shot dead.

The incident convinced Lee that he must go into hiding. Accompanied by a small band of followers, he fled into a nearby wilderness appropriately named Wildcat Thicket. From there, Lee spread the word that he intended to give the Union League and the U.S. government a war. That prospect brought a number of ex-soldier volunteers into his wilderness camp.

Once his wound had healed sufficiently for him to sit a horse, Lee unleashed a reign of terror on enemies real and imagined. He led raid after raid that resulted in the deaths of scores of Union Leaguers. He set up a military-like headquarters in the almost impenetrable tangle of Wildcat Thicket, posting sentries and establishing an intelligence network among sympathetic farmers in the region. The U.S. Army could not make a move without Lee being informed.

When a company of soldiers arrived to flush Lee and his men from Wildcat Thicket, it was ambushed. The resulting casualties caused Army officials to rethink their strategy. By then it was apparent that a large force would be required to capture the former Confederates in their wilderness fortress. Also obvious was that substantial casualties would result from any large-scale assault on Wildcat Thicket. A decision was made to contain Lee rather than attack him. He was branded an outlaw, and a $1,000 reward was placed on his head.

The reward inspired bounty hunters from near and far to enter the thicket looking for Lee. One by one their bullet-riddled bodies were found dumped on roadsides near Pilot Grove as a warning to others to stay away. As months and then years passed, Lee and his men made occasional forays from their wilderness fortress to secure supplies or wreak vengeance on Union Leaguers for acts committed against Lee sympathizers. Meanwhile, the government continued to increase the reward on Lee until it reached $10,000, a fortune in the South during reconstruction. The reward finally produced the desired result.

In the pre-dawn hours on the morning of May 24, 1869, a Captain Campbell of the U.S. Army led a company of soldiers down a narrow road on the outskirts of Wildcat Thicket. In the darkness, he deployed his men in the woods beside the road. The captain was acting on a tip that Bob Lee would be traveling the road that morning. It was almost nine o'clock when a lone rider, trailed by a pack horse, came up the road. As he drew near, the woods erupted with gunfire.

★

**PART
THREE**
*Scandals
and
Scoundrels*

127

That's
Not
in My
American
History
Book

Bob Lee tumbled from his saddle. He was dead when he hit the ground. Upon examination of the body, it became apparent that he was prepared for a long trip. There was a large amount of gold in his saddlebags and belt. He was dressed for travel, and the pack horse carried provisions for a journey. It was speculated that he had been departing for Mexico when he was killed.

A rumor quickly spread that Lee was betrayed by a local farmer he had trusted. The following morning, the farmer was found dead.

Lee's leaderless men scattered. Some disappeared, never to be seen in the area again. Others were identified as outlaws and hunted down by the authorities. One who escaped was Dick Johnson, one of Lee's most daring and vicious lieutenants. For two years he remained in hiding. Then one day he boldly appeared in Pilot Grove and announced that he was there to "kill the Fowl," which was the rebels' nickname for Peacock. Because of his reputation as a killer, no one dared challenge Johnson.

Lewis Peacock remained holed up in his house, apparently hopeful that Johnson would leave town before he had a chance to carry out his threat. But the morning after Johnson's arrival, Peacock made a fatal mistake when he stepped onto his back porch to fetch stove wood. He was shot from ambush, and Dick Johnson was never seen again in Pilot Grove.

The final victim of the conflict was Daniel Lee, Bob's father. He was riding home from the town of Bonham when he was shot from ambush. The authorities claimed he was the victim of a robbery, but no one around Pilot Grove believed it.

It has been estimated that as many as two hundred men died in the four years of the standoff. Shortly before his death, Bob Lee confided to friends that he personally had killed forty-two men. Although forgotten by history, the events of that time are still a part of the region's lore. And, more than 130 years after the deaths of Bob Lee and Lewis Peacock, there remains an undercurrent of animosity among the descendants of those on the opposing sides.

The Difficult Mrs. Lincoln

There has never been another first lady like Mary Todd Lincoln. Her violent fits of temper, often played out in public, are well known. She was a shrew and a hellcat and when riled, totally beyond control. She frequently abused her husband, physically and verbally. Beyond doubt she was mentally disturbed. Her bizarre behavior was the talk of Washington, D.C., and a source of continuing embarrassment, sadness, and concern to the president.

However, only in recent years has it come to light that Mary Lincoln also was a thief. The revelation came about with the release of diaries that had been hidden away at the Illinois Historical Library in Springfield for more than a century. The diaries, penned by U.S. Senator Owen Hickman Browning of Illinois during Lincoln's presidency, were hidden from the public by library officials in an effort to protect the image of the former first lady.

What the diaries reveal is a first lady engaged in a blatant pattern of misappropriation of public funds and, in some instances, outright thievery. At a time when the Union was straining under the economic burden of financing a prolonged war, Mrs. Lincoln was running up astronomical bills on the White House expense account. Among the items she purchased at government expense were 300 pairs of expensive kid gloves. At a time when Union soldiers were fighting and dying for $13 a month, Mrs. Lincoln was purchasing dresses that cost up to $2,000 each, including some that were never worn. And, when she left the White House, Mrs. Lincoln took just about anything that was not nailed down.

There is little disagreement among historians that the diaries are an accurate portrayal of the dark side of Mary Lincoln. Senator Browning was probably the closest friend President Lincoln had during his years in the White House and, in some instances, the diaries are even sympathetic to Mrs. Lincoln.

★

That's
Not
in My
American
History
Book

130

As if a Civil War weren't enough Mary Todd Lincoln misappropriated government funds to cover her debts. *National Archives & Records Administration*

Upon the senator's death, his family donated the diaries to the Illinois Historical Library with the stipulation that those parts referring to Mrs. Lincoln's behavior never be released to the public. Library officials adhered to the family's wishes until 1994, when pressure from historians finally forced their release.

Lincoln's early biographers went to great lengths to protect the image of Mrs. Lincoln. In recent years, Michael Burlingame, a professor of history at Connecticut College, himself a Lincoln biographer, has plowed through notes taken by writers who knew the Lincolns. From their notes he has gleaned information the interviewers considered improper for publication. Among Burlingame's findings of physical abuse:

"Once she got mad and threw a cup of scalding coffee in his face. Another time she was peeling potatoes, got mad . . . and started throwing potatoes at him. She even smacked him in the face with a piece of firewood."

When the Lincolns were still living in Illinois, a neighbor looked out of his window one morning and saw five-foot-two Mary Lincoln, clutching a kitchen knife over her head, chasing her six-foot-four husband down the road. When they met some of their neighbors on the road, an embarrassed Lincoln stopped and wrestled the knife from his wife.

Such was Mary Lincoln's reputation that many in Washington did not want to be seen socially with her. On the final day of Lincoln's life, no less than fourteen people turned down invitations to accompany the president and first lady to the Ford's Theater that night. It originally was planned that Gen. Ulysses Grant and his wife, Julia, would join the Lincolns at the theater. But Julia Grant would have nothing to do with the first lady. Two weeks earlier, when the Grants were guests of the Lincolns during the inspection of a ship, Julia Grant had become fatigued and decided to rest by sitting on a coil of rope. That prompted Mary Lincoln to begin yelling at her:

"How dare you sit in the presence of the wife of the president!" she admonished the startled Mrs. Grant.

Mrs. Lincoln not only was obsessed with expensive clothing, but her rather daring sense of fashion was a subject for gossip as well. Her insistence on wearing revealing gowns sometimes caused conflict with the president. On one occasion when she selected a gown with a long train and plunging neckline for a White House reception, the president tactfully suggested the outfit might be more attractive if some of the fabric from the train was used "a little closer to the head." The remark sent the indignant first lady into a rage. The disagreement was concluded when Mrs. Lincoln announced she would attend the reception in the dress whether or not her husband chose to accompany her. Lincoln dutifully escorted his wife to the reception, and Mrs. Lincoln's plunging neckline was the talk of the town for days.

In spite of his wife's mental state, Lincoln remained a devoted husband to the end. He once confessed to Browning: "I'm convinced the peculiarities of my wife's behavior are the result of partial insanity." A rumor circulated in Washington and persisted through the years that Mary Lincoln's mental state resulted from a social disease contracted from her husband early in their marriage. Supposedly, the president blamed himself for her condition and devoted himself to caring for her.

★

PART
THREE
*Scandals
and
Scoundrels*

131

That's
Not
in My
American
History
Book

Their son, Todd Lincoln, did not have his father's patience. In 1875, unable to cope with the behavior of his mother, he had her placed in a mental institution. She remained there for six months before being released. A tragic figure, she died in 1882 at the home of her sister in Springfield in the same house where she had been living when she became Abe Lincoln's bride, forty years before.

When she was in Washington, one of Mrs. Lincoln's favorite activities was to ride around town in the presidential carriage while snubbing the socially elite of the city. On the afternoon of the day Lincoln died, he canceled all of his appointments to humor Mrs. Lincoln and accompany her on one of her rides around the streets of Washington in the presidential carriage.

Did John Wilkes Booth Escape?

On a winter morning in 1871, in the little town of Granbury, Texas, a saloon keeper named F. J. Gordon went out to check on one of his employees who had been ill for several days. The man he was going to visit was John St. Helen, the bartender at Gordon's saloon.

St. Helen lived in a boarding house on the outskirts of town. Upon entering St. Helen's room, Gordon immediately became concerned. He found the man in a terrible physical state. Flushed with fever and semi-delirious, St. Helen was convinced he was dying and asked Gordon to bring a clergyman to his bedside before it was too late. Gordon left him there to go find a preacher.

Although St. Helen had lived in Granbury for almost four years, he remained something of a mystery. It was known that he had relatives living in the area, yet he seldom associated with them. His attire was a source of curiosity from the day he arrived. He was a dapper dresser—or, at least, dapper for Granbury. He was well spoken and obviously well educated.

St. Helen kept to himself, rarely attending or expressing interest in local social events. He was not unfriendly; but beyond tipping his hat or occasionally engaging in brief conversation, he did not socialize. Physically, he was slender of build and walked with a slight limp, which locals assumed resulted from a wound received in the recent war. He was always well groomed.

Gordon liked St. Helen. He had befriended him when others had not and offered him a job when others would not. St. Helen had proven himself a good bartender, and Gordon became the closest thing he had to a friend in Granbury. Beyond his job, St. Helen's only other interest seemed to be the horse races at the local track. Gordon owned a string of racehorses and, upon observing that St. Helen was an excellent horseman, prevailed on him to help with the training of the animals.

When Gordon returned to St. Helen's room with the clergy-

⭐

**That's
Not
in My
American
History
Book**

134

man that morning, they found him in a state of obvious delirium. St. Helen began a rambling confession that made little sense to them. Finally, he revealed that his name was not John St. Helen. He said it was John Wilkes Booth.

Although skeptical, Gordon listened as his bartender described how he had hidden the pistol he used to shoot the president. He said that he placed it in the outside corner of a house where he once resided. Gordon was familiar with the house, and upon leaving St. Helen's boarding house, went there expecting not to find anything. What he found was a cloth bundle exactly where the bartender said it would be. Unfolding it, he found a newspaper wrapped around a chamois belt containing seven cartridges and a Derringer pistol. The newspaper was six years old. Its front page carried accounts of the assassination.

Not knowing what he should do with the items, Gordon took them home and hid them. When he returned to the boarding house to check on St. Helen, he was gone. He was never seen again in Granbury.

Gordon kept his secret for almost twenty years before he finally contacted the authorities. Put in touch with federal agents, he told his story and offered to show them the pistol, chamois belt, and newspaper. They thanked him and said that since the case was closed, they had no interest in pursuing an investigation.

Gordon died in 1918 with the items still in his possession. His daughter, Mrs. Frances Gordon Bryan, to whom he had often repeated the story, kept the Derringer, belt, and newspaper for many years. She passed on the story to her children and grandchildren.

In 1965, on the occasion of the hundredth anniversary of Lincoln's assassination, the local newspaper published an article about the St. Helen mystery. It was picked up by the Associated Press and distributed to newspapers nationwide. The source of information for the article was Mrs. J. C. Porter of Wichita Falls, Texas, granddaughter of F. J. Gordon. She recounted the story told to her by her mother and exhibited a pistol and chamois belt with seven cartridges. She explained that there had been a newspaper with the items, but it was lost years before.

Upon examination, the Derringer turned out to be an 1857 model manufactured by the Brown Company of Massachusetts.

Could it be possible John Wilkes Booth escaped and fled to Texas after assassinating President Lincoln? The scenario is most unlikely—yet, over the years, there has remained just enough fuel to feed a flicker of doubt.

John St. Helen?
John Wilkes Booth, supposedly killed after Lincoln's assassination, may have escaped to Texas.
National Archives & Records Administration

In the wake of the Lincoln assassination, conspiracy rumors swept the country. And, as in the case of the Kennedy assassination a century later, those responsible for investigating Lincoln's death generated more questions than answers.

There was never any doubt that John Wilkes Booth shot the president. The question was always who was behind it. Everyone knew there had to be a conspiracy. Many in the North thought Confederate President Jefferson Davis had ordered it. In the South it was believed radical abolitionists were behind it because of Lincoln's lenient approach to reconstruction in the South. It was blamed on Democrats desirous of putting Vice President Andrew Johnson in the White House. It was blamed on a network of Southern spies operating at the highest levels of the federal government. There was speculation that U.S. Secretary of War Edwin Stanton was involved, and one rumor had it that the Catholic Church was behind the assassination and the Pope had ordered Lincoln's death. Few paused to consider the possibility that a

That's
Not
in My
American
History
Book

frustrated stage actor might have been playing out the most dramatic role of his life.

Twelve days after Lincoln was shot, a Union cavalry patrol trapped two men in a tobacco barn on Richard Garrett's farm not far from Washington. The soldiers ordered the men inside to come out and surrender. One of the men emerged. He was David Herold, a mentally retarded, part-time employee at a Washington drug store. He would be charged as a co-conspirator in the assassination and hanged. The second man remained inside the barn, refusing to surrender.

The soldiers set the barn on fire to force the man outside. As fire consumed the structure, a soldier named Boston Corbett peered through a crack in the wall and saw a figure illuminated by the glow of the flames. Disobeying a direct order, Corbett raised his cavalry pistol and fired. The bullet penetrated the man's lower neck, striking the spine.

Lt. Luther Baker also had been watching the man through cracks in the wall. He insisted the man had put down his weapon and was coming out to surrender when he was shot. He had Corbett placed under arrest for disobeying an order.

The soldiers dragged the man from the burning barn and carried him to the Garrett farmhouse. They placed him on the porch, and from that point accounts begin to differ. There were reports the man was alive and made a dramatic confession before dying, imploring those present to "Tell my mother I died for my country" and finally holding up his hands and muttering, "Useless, useless." Others reported there was no confession, because the man was either dead or unconscious when placed on the porch. There were reports he was badly burned. Others insisted he was not burned.

Booth was a vain man, always immaculately dressed, neatly shaven, and never a hair out of place. The man on the porch was described as "a hideous sight," dirty and disheveled, with a heavy, scraggly beard. According to the official report, Booth died about seven o'clock that morning, some three hours after the shooting in the burning barn.

Rumors that the man killed at Garrett's farm was not really Booth began to spread almost immediately. In all probability, the body of the man on the porch was that of Booth. Yet, nagging questions remain.

Why, almost two weeks after the assassination, was Booth still in the vicinity of Washington, D.C.? The leg he broke leaping from Lincoln's box onto the stage had been set, and he should have been able to travel. Is it possible he had the intelligence to organize a conspiracy to assassinate the president and members of his cabinet, but did not have the foresight to plot his own escape?

Booth had meticulously planned the assassination, going to the trouble of boring holes in a wall so that Lincoln could be observed in his box and fixing a door so that he was able to enter the box and then block it so it could not be opened. He had arranged for a stagehand to have a horse waiting for him outside the theater.

Considering all of his planning, it might be assumed that Booth would be intelligent enough to have a strategy for escape or at least a fresh mount waiting for him beyond the Potomac River. Failing that, he surely could have borrowed a horse from one of the many Southern sympathizers in the area. After all, according to the government, Booth was a spy with contacts in Virginia. The man with the beard and David Herold were seen walking around the countryside and sleeping in barns for two days before authorities were notified and they were trapped at Garrett's farm. Could Booth have walked around for two days on a broken leg?

Other questions arise. Was it possible that Booth could have grown a full beard in only twelve days? Why was there ever a question about his identity? Booth was a famous actor earning $20,000 a year performing on Washington and New York stages. His face had been in newspapers and on placards. A week before speaking at Gettysburg, Lincoln himself had gone to see Booth perform in the play, *The Marble Heart.*

At Garrett's farm, the body was sewn into a saddle blanket, placed on a wagon, and taken to Belle Plain, Virginia. There it was placed on the steamer *John S. Ide* and taken to Alexandria, Virginia, before being sent on to a Navy yard on the Potomac. Some eight witnesses were brought there to identify the body—all carefully selected by Secretary of War Edwin Stanton. Among them were a doctor and Booth's dentist. The autopsy, performed by U.S. Army Surgeon Gen. Joseph K. Barnes, consisted of little more than an examination of the neck wound.

On Stanton's orders, the body then was taken to a remote, abandoned federal penitentiary on the banks of the Potomac at Greenleaf Point. There, in what had been the prison exercise room, in an atmosphere of secrecy, a section of brick floor was removed, the body was placed in a grave, and the brick floor cemented back in place.

Why was Stanton determined to personally control every aspect of the identification process, the investigation, and the result-

That's
Not
in My
American
History
Book

138

ing military trial? Why were photographs not taken during the autopsy? Why the secrecy surrounding the burial? And finally, the most important question of all: When Stanton had Booth's personal effects brought to him, why did he keep Booth's diary—and why, when it was finally released, were pages missing?

The questions do not end with the deposit of a body beneath the floor of an abandoned penitentiary. There are questions surrounding the assassination itself. The most obvious one is why Lincoln was left virtually unprotected that night. John Parker, Lincoln's personal bodyguard, and Booth were both drinking separately at Taltavul's Saloon next door to the theater until 10:15 that evening. That is when Booth departed, walked next door, and shot the president.

Why were Booth's co-conspirators such an odd assortment of misfits, none of whom seemed to have strong political agendas? George Atzerodt was a German immigrant who could barely speak English. David Herold was retarded. Lewis Powell was a Confederate turncoat who had proclaimed allegiance to the Union, and Mary Surratt's only crimes seemed to be that she had the misfortune to own the boarding house where the conspirators met and to be the mother of Booth's chief conspirator, John Surratt. Why would a famous actor like Booth even have occasion to socialize with such characters?

In 1869 the body was removed from its secret location at Greenleaf Point and transferred to Green Mount Cemetery at Baltimore, Maryland. In 1991, the television show *Unsolved Mysteries* produced a documentary strongly suggesting that the body in the Baltimore cemetery was not that of the assassin. That prompted several descendants of Booth to file a lawsuit to exhume the body for forensic study and positive identification. After four days of testimony, the judge dismissed the petition, citing a high probability that the body could not be properly identified even if it was exhumed.

Was Booth a pawn in a wider conspiracy? Did someone other than Booth die at Richard Garrett's farm that morning? Did Secretary Stanton have knowledge of the assassination plot beforehand and let it take place? Is the body resting beneath the headstone at Green Mount Cemetery in Baltimore that of John Wilkes Booth?

And there remains one final unanswered question. Who was John St. Helen?

Raising a Glass to General Custer

The rumor has persisted for well over a century. Were Gen. George A. Custer's soldiers either drunk or suffering a collective hangover that fateful day they were massacred at Little Big Horn?

The speculation began when Sioux veterans of the legendary battle reported finding numerous canteens containing whiskey instead of water on the bodies of Custer's soldiers. Supposedly, the U.S. Army, already smarting from criticism over the conduct of the campaign, covered up the fact that the men of the 7th Cavalry had been drinking the night before their ill-fated meeting with the Sioux.

That memorable encounter took place on June 25, 1876. Many questions about the events of that day remain unanswered, but this much we do know:

The flamboyant Custer and his 7th Cavalry were part of a U.S. Army force ordered to search out and subdue tribes under the leadership of Chief Sitting Bull, the religious leader of the Sioux. As Custer and his men closed in on the Indians, he had no way of knowing that Sitting Bull had brought together a great gathering of tribes that included the Cheyenne at an encampment on the banks of the Little Big Horn River in what is now Montana.

As Custer approached the encampment, he ignored reports from scouts that a large number of Indians were ahead. His only concern was to be the first to engage the Sioux, so that he might reap the rewards of victory—and perhaps a presidential nomination in the process. Arrogant to a fault, Custer was confident his cavalry could defeat any number of Indians. His greatest fear that day was that the enemy might flee from him and get away. To prevent that possibility, he split his command and sent some 300 troops under Maj. Marcus Reno to circle around the encampment and cut off any retreat. However, retreat was the last thing the Sioux had in mind.

⭐

That's
Not
in My
American
History
Book

(Left)
**The dashing general
dashed**
Gen. George Armstrong
Custer led the 7th
Cavalry into a deadly
ambush. *National Archives
& Records Administration*

(Right)
**Aftermath of the
massacre**
A pile of bones attests
to the violent conflict
at Little Big Horn.
*National Archives &
Records Administration*

As Custer and the remaining 264 cavalrymen under his direct command approached the encampment, some 4,000 angry warriors descended on them. Seldom mentioned in published accounts of the battle is that many of the Indians were better armed than Custer's troops. Some had repeating rifles, while Custer's men were armed with single-shot rifles that tended to overheat after repeated firing.

It is believed the battle lasted less than two hours. When the massacre was complete, the Indians looted the battlefield. Numerous canteens containing whiskey were among the loot.

Dashing and daring, Custer had a reputation for being somewhat cavalier when it came to discipline. Almost anything went in Custer's camp, except desertion. In an earlier campaign, he had ordered several executions to halt a rash of desertions. Ironically, Custer himself was then court-martialed and temporarily suspended from the Army for leaving his post to visit his wife. Only intervention by his old friend, Gen. Philip Sheridan, saved his career.

Whether Custer condoned drinking in the ranks or simply ignored it is not known, but the practice appears to have been widespread enough that it could not have escaped his attention. What is known is that Custer's second in command, Major Reno, was a heavy drinker. In fact, he secured a full keg of whiskey to accom-

★

PART
THREE
*Scandals
and
Scoundrels*

141

pany him on the mission when the 7th Cavalry set out to locate the Sioux. Just four days before the massacre, Custer's troops met a steamboat on the Rosebud River. In addition to supplies, the steamboat carried a large quantity of whiskey, and many of the soldiers replenished their supply of spirits at that time.

The conduct of Major Reno on the day of the battle has been a subject for debate over the years. Commanding more than half of Custer's troops, Reno circled around the encampment as ordered. Upon being attacked, he immediately directed his men to retreat into a defensive position, leaving Custer to face almost the full force of the Sioux attack. He ignored pleas to go to Custer's aid, refusing to budge from his position.

Whether the major's decisions that day were clouded by the consumption of alcohol will never be known. But reports indicate that while his men held their position that afternoon, Major Reno was drinking heavily. His subordinates reported that when they were besieged that night, he was intoxicated to the point of being irrational. In defense of Reno, it should be pointed out that, drunk or sober, if he had gone to Custer's aid the outcome might have been the same—with the added possibility his own command would have been massacred.

At the time Custer began his campaign against the Sioux, he

That's
Not
in My
American
History
Book

was something of a national folk hero, perhaps as much in his own mind as in that of the public. As the "Boy General" in the Civil War, he established a well-publicized, if not fully earned, reputation as a daring cavalry officer. His reckless and sometimes ill-advised actions caused his superiors to cringe, but Custer inevitably garnered praise from an adoring press.

As he began that final campaign, Custer had serious ambitions to become a candidate for president of the United States. The only blemish on his record was the court-martial for desertion, and he was determined to overshadow that with a victory over the Sioux. Custer was convinced that his popularity was such that he needed only one impressive victory in the field to boost him into the White House. However, instead of being cheered on Pennsylvania Avenue, Custer and his ambitions were drowned in a chorus of war cries on a remote hillside overlooking the Little Big Horn River.

In spite of all the unanswered questions about the events of that day, there is one certainty. Since 1876, the Sioux have never again had so much influence in the presidential nominating process.

The Teen "Angels" of Salem

Colonial Salem, Massachusetts, was a rather dull place for teenage girls with active imaginations. It was a Puritan village, and beyond chores and church there was little to do in Salem in the 1690s. But that was before the girls discovered Tituba.

Tituba was a slave from the West Indies who worked in the kitchen of the rectory of Reverend Samuel Parris, the village minister. She was a spellbinding storyteller, and the young and impressionable girls of Salem were drawn to her tales of distant places and exotic people. During drab winter days, the girls would sit wide-eyed in the rectory kitchen, listening to stories that became increasingly bizarre. With dramatic effect, Tituba related West Indies tales of sorcery, voodoo, witchcraft, and other dark and foreboding practices.

The elders of Salem were mystified when their daughters began to exhibit strange patterns of behavior. Some of the girls complained of faintness. Sometimes they would swoon and fall to the floor, and the concern expressed by their parents seemed only to inspire even more outlandish behavior. Soon, some of the young girls of Salem were lapsing into hysterical fits that included kicking and screaming.

Fathers and mothers were horrified. Farmers left their fields unattended to keep watchful eyes on their daughters. Mothers wept and prayed for deliverance of their children from the evil that was possessing them.

The behavior became progressively worse. The girls screamed that they were being choked and bitten. They cried out that unseen hands were trying to strangle them, said they could smell brimstone, and went into convulsions. They engaged in conversations with apparitions. Their eyes rolled and their bodies went limp as though life itself had been drained from them.

For the elders of Salem, there could be only one explanation.

★

That's
Not
in My
American
History
Book

They lived in a place in which everyone believed, without question, that Satan was an instigator of evil deeds. It had become obvious to them that Satan and his forces were possessing their daughters.

Under questioning, the girls confided to their parents that "witches" were casting spells upon them. With the assistance of the girls, church leaders began seeking out and identifying suspected witches who, they were convinced, were disciples of the devil. Most of the so-called witches were elderly women. One by one they were hauled into court, where the star witnesses against them were the young girls of Salem.

As a result of the Salem witch trials, the girls were elevated to the status of "angels" doing the work of the Lord. Their testimony included demonstrations that became more and more bizarre as the trials progressed. For those accused there was no possible defense. One by one, they were found guilty and hanged.

As the trials continued, the accusations of the Salem angels became so unbelievable that even the church elders began to doubt their veracity. By the time the hysteria subsided and the trials were stopped, the Salem witch hunt had gone on for more than two years and spread to nearby communities. Twenty convicted witches were hanged. The purge reached such frenetic madness that two dogs were found guilty of witchcraft and hanged.

How could such an outrage happen? Indeed, what did possess the Puritan maidens of Salem to inspire such odd behavior? It would be almost 300 years after the trials when the answer finally emerged. It came not from a musty journal, but from a chemistry laboratory. The answer is ergotism. Some historians are convinced the Salem angels were under the influence of a mind-altering drug present in ergot, a fungus that grows in moldy grain.

Ergotism outbreaks, affecting entire regions, were common in Europe in the Middle Ages. But there was little knowledge of the hallucinogenic effects of moldy grain in seventeenth-century America. In modern times ergot has been used to produce drugs for medical purposes, such as those used for the treatment of migraine headaches. But if consumed in its pure state, it is a potent toxin that can cause disorientation, hallucinations, and even death.

There is little doubt the drug, playing upon young innocent minds filled with Tituba's hair-raising stories of sorcery, voodoo, and witchcraft, might prove a tragic combination. But why were only the girls affected and not others? The most likely scenario is that Tibuta introduced the girls to the mind-altering wonders found in moldy grain. Her knowledge of sorcery likely included an understanding of various toxins and their sources.

Did she introduce the girls to ergot in the form of a potion prepared to enhance their sensibilities while they listened to her stories? Considering the duration of the witch hunt, she probably introduced them to the grain and the girls continued to consume it on their own in greater and greater quantities. Was Tituba a willing accomplice to the madness that consumed twenty innocent lives? It is more likely she was only a naive kitchen slave trying to entertain a group of young girls with frightening tales of the supernatural. The answers to the entire bizarre affair are long buried with the teen angels of Salem.

PART
THREE
*Scandals
and
Scoundrels*

145

PART FOUR

From Mutton Head to Slick Willie

Little-Known Facts about Famous People

*Could it be true that a U.S. president was blinded in one eye while sparring
with a professional boxer in the White House, or that Ben Franklin almost
killed himself trying to electrocute a turkey? Strange, bizarre? Yes, but true.
Our history abounds with astonishing anecdotes about famous people,
stories that somehow became lost in time. For example, few realize that
"Old Mutton Head" was the father of our country, Abraham Lincoln was
a champion handball player, and Woodrow Wilson drew up football
formations, variations of which are still used today. These are the stories
your history teacher never told you about our nation's icons.*

Gipper, Granny, and Tricky Dicky

Presidential Nicknames

Fortunate is the man who lives out his years without acquiring a derogatory nickname. Most of our presidents were not so lucky.

In fact, if the study of nicknames was a part of traditional education, students today would know that "Mutton Head" Washington was the father of our country, "Long Tom" Jefferson penned the Declaration of Independence, and "Handsome Frank" Pierce approved the Gadsden Purchase.

These are but a few of the little-known nicknames of our presidents. They all had them, from "Useless" Grant to "Gipper" Reagan, from "Ole Granny" Harrison to "Slick Willie" Clinton.

It all began, appropriately enough, with George Washington. He was known affectionately as "The Old Fox" and the "Sage of Mount Vernon." But when John Adams became angry at him, he referred to the father of the nation as Mutton Head. Thomas Jefferson had yet another name for Washington. When he became peeved at the president, he called him "His Pomposity."

Adams and Jefferson were not without nicknames of their own—several of which they called each other during their political battles before old age finally forged a bond of friendship between them. Adams was known as "Old Sink or Swim" because of his uncompromising nature and "The Monarch" for his belief in a strong federal government. He also was called "His Rotundity" in reference to his diminutive statue and rather ample girth. Jefferson was "Long Tom" or "The Pen," and in the tradition of Washington, "The Sage of Monticello."

James Madison was known as "Short Stack," but the sobriquet referred not so much to his stature (at five-four he was our shortest president) as to his temperament. To Washington's socially elite, he was "Dolly's Husband." His buxom wife was the toast of the town for her lavish receptions. He also was called the "Father of the Constitution" for his contribution to that document.

That's
Not
in My
American
History
Book

James Monroe, our fifth president, was "The Last of the Cocked Hats," a nickname earned for his old-fashioned clothing, gentlemanly bearing, and sometimes lofty manner, rather than for his headdress. Jefferson said of him, "If Monroe's soul was turned inside out, you would not find a spot on it."

John Quincy Adams, the son of John Adams, could not escape being referred to as "The President's Son" even after he became president. He also was called "Old Eloquent" for his ability to turn a phrase.

Andrew Jackson was "The Duel Fighter," "Hero of New Orleans," "Old Rugged," and, of course, "Old Hickory." Jackson also was called "Caesar of the White House"—or sometimes just "Caesar"—by his enemies, who were legion.

Diminutive Martin Van Buren was called "The Little Magician" or the "Wizard of Kinderhook" because of his political sleight of hand. Military hero William Henry Harrison was "Ole Tippecanoe" because of his victory over the Indians at the Tippecanoe River. He also was called "Ole Granny" because he sometimes acted like one.

John Tyler was given the nickname "His Accidency" after ascending to the White House when Harrison died in office. He also was called the "White House Romeo" after he became the first

Mutton Head triumphant George Washington enters New York to the cheers of its citizens. *National Archives & Records Administration*

Our American Caesar Andrew Jackson earned numerous nicknames, including "Caesar of the White House." *Metropolitan Museum of Art, Dick Fund*

president to marry while in office. His bride was a beautiful young widow named Julia Gardiner, who was being courted by several handsome and wealthy suitors when she chose Tyler, who was thirty years her senior. Descended from a wealthy New York family, Julia's own nickname was "The Rose of Long Island."

James Knox Polk, our eleventh president, was called the "Napoleon of the Stump" and also was known as "Young Hickory."

Scrappy military hero Zachary Taylor was "Old Rough 'n' Ready." His friends called him "Zack." His attempt to compromise the slavery debate between North and South resulted in his being called many names that are not printable in this volume.

Millard Fillmore was called "Bathtub Millard" after he had indoor plumbing installed in the White House. "Handsome Frank" was the nickname given Franklin Pierce for his classic features. His enemies called him "The Drunkard" because of his extreme fondness for spirits. He also was called "Purse" for reasons not recorded. James Buchanan was "Ten Cent Jimmy" and "The Bachelor President."

Abraham Lincoln was "The Rail Splitter," "Honest Abe," and "The Great Emancipator." Andrew Johnson was known as "Sir Veto" due to his use of that presidential prerogative in the tumultuous years following Lincoln's assassination. Impeached by the House of Representatives, "Sir Veto" underwent a Senate trial and managed to keep his job by a single vote.

Probably no president had more nicknames that were both praiseworthy and derogatory than Ulysses S. Grant. As a Civil War hero, he was called "Unconditional Surrender" Grant. As probably our most inept president, he became "Useless" Grant.

President Rutherford B. Hayes was nicknamed "His Fraudulency" after Republican power brokers managed to steal the election that put him in the White House. He also was referred to as the "President de Facto."

James A. Garfield was called "The Dark Horse" and "The Martyr." He also was "The Horseshoe Pitcher" because of his obsession with the sport. Chester A. Arthur was known as "The Dude" because of his dapper dress. He was "Chet" to his friends; the newspapers referred to him, rather grandly, as "America's First Gentleman."

Rotund Grover Cleveland was known as "The Stuffed Prophet," but his campaign workers liked to refer to him as the

⭐

**That's
Not
in My
American
History
Book**

152

"Man of Destiny." Benjamin Harrison was called "Kid Gloves" for his reluctance to engage in political conflict. He also was "The Hoosier." William McKinley was nicknamed the "White House Virgin" or simply, "The Virgin." We can only assume the reference was to his political innocence. His supporters were more kind. They called him "The Bonaparte of Politics."

Theodore "Teddy" Roosevelt was nicknamed "Old Dynamo" and "The Rough Rider." He was called "T. R." by his friends. William Howard Taft (our largest president) was referred to as "Jumbo Bill" and "Old Heavy Cargo." Our most traveled president until that time, he also was known as "The Globe Trotter." Woodrow Wilson was "The Professor" or "The Scholar."

Warren Gamaliel Harding was called the "Broom Closet Lover," because that is where he met his mistress. Legend has it the closet had two doors so his mistress could escape out of one when his wife approached the other. Some referred to him as "Poor Slob." It is not known if this sobriquet resulted from traits of personality or the fact that he had to endure the burden of a middle name like Gamaliel.

Calvin Coolidge was nicknamed "Red" for the hue of his hair, not his politics. Herbert Hoover was "Herbie" to close friends (who became fewer with the onset of the Great Depression) and "Two-Chickens-in-Every-Pot Herbie" to his detractors. His name also became associated with the cardboard shantytowns that sprang up beside rail yards during the Depression. They were called "Hoovervilles."

Franklin D. Roosevelt (FDR for short) was called the "White House Houdini," after famous escape artist Harry Houdini, for his ability to bedazzle his political opponents. He also was referred to as "His Majesty" and "King Roosevelt" because of his four-term reign in the White House.

Harry S. Truman had many nicknames, but most of them cannot be repeated in polite company. He was called "Give-em-Hell-Harry" after an admirer was inspired to shout that phrase from a crowd during the 1948 presidential campaign. He was known as "Sassy Pants" and "Old Mulehead" (in reference to his Missouri background) and "Dammit Harry" because he often prefaced what he was going to say with "dammit."

Dwight David Eisenhower, whose name was shortened to "Ike" by the nation's newspaper headline writers, was called "Do Nothing Ike," "The Golfer," and "World Mangler."

John F. Kennedy was nicknamed "Jack." He was called "The

Hero" by staff and friends because of his heroics following the sinking of the PT boat he commanded during World War II. He might have been called "White House Romeo," but the name already was taken.

Lyndon B. Johnson was tagged with the ironic nickname "Landslide Lyndon" after he defeated an opponent by 87 votes for a seat in the U.S. Senate in an election tainted by voter fraud. He also was known as "Huffy Puffy Lyndon" when he lost his temper, which was often.

Richard Nixon became "Tricky Dicky," and his detractors posed the question, "Would you buy a used car from this man?" Gerald A. Ford was called "Jerry." He liked to refer to himself as "Gerald A. Ford, not a Lincoln." He also acquired the nickname "Twinkle Toes" because of the frequency with which he tripped himself up physically and politically.

What does the "U. S." stand for? Ulysses S. Grant gained nicknames from both admirers and detractors alike. *National Archives & Records Administration*

Give-'Em-Hell-Harry Harry S. Truman's large collection of nicknames often stemmed from his irascible character. *Harry S. Truman Library*

Jimmy Carter, whose childhood nickname was "Hot Shot," grew up to become "Pepsodent Jimmy" for his dazzling smile and "Peanut Jimmy" because he grew peanuts on his Georgia farm.

Ronald Reagan was known as "The Great Communicator" for his ability to charm an audience. But he was more commonly known as "The Gipper," so named for his portrayal of football hero George Gipp in the movie *Knute Rockne: All American.* Some

That's
Not
in My
American
History
Book

cynical critics in the Washington press corps called him "The Ripper," after Rip Van Winkle, because of the president's habit of nodding off during meetings and public events.

George Bush was called "Poppy" when he captained the Yale baseball team, and it stuck with him for many years. Bush, a World War II veteran, was older than his college teammates, prompting them to hang the "Poppy" label on him. He later would be known as "Read My Lips Bush." He earned that one when, during the presidential campaign of 1988 he said, "Read my lips—No new taxes." Upon becoming president, he caved in to political pressure and agreed to a tax increase, whereupon the nation's taxpayers rewarded him with early retirement.

William Jefferson (Bill) Clinton was "Bubba" to family and boyhood friends back in Arkansas. He later became "Slick Willie" for his ability to talk his way out of political crises after he had talked his way into them. He was remarkably successful at this right up until he was impeached by the House of Representatives and held in contempt of court by a federal judge for lying. Political cartoonists sometimes depicted him as "Pinocchio" as a result of his continuing struggle with the truth.

Will future presidents continue the nickname tradition established by the likes of "Mutton Head" and "Slick Willie?" Is there another "Ten Cent Jimmy" or "Give-em-Hell-Harry" on the horizon? Only time will tell.

Benedict Arnold, American Hero

F. Scott Fitzgerald once said, "Show me a hero and I'll write you a tragedy." Never have Fitzgerald's words been more apropos than when applied to Benedict Arnold.

Before he became a traitor to America, Arnold was a hero. He saved the American Revolution. In the most important battle in the War for Independence, Arnold defied his commander and won a great victory. If Arnold had not done so—if he had not been at Saratoga, New York, at that defining moment in history—there might not have been a United States of America.

To understand the significance of the events that took place at Saratoga in 1777, it should be noted that Sir Edward Creasy, the foremost military historian of the nineteenth century, listed Saratoga among the fifteen most important battles in the history of humankind. It was the battle (actually a series of battles) that turned the tide in America's struggle for independence. Even more significant, if the colonials had been defeated there, they almost certainly would have lost the war.

With the outbreak of hostilities in America, both sides anticipated a rapid conclusion to the struggle. George Washington predicted the conflict would last no more than six months. It lasted six years.

The British plan for a quick victory was simple in concept—blockade the coast, control the Hudson River, and win the war. The British planned to clear the Hudson River Valley of rebel forces and build a string of forts from its upper lakes to New York City. Once that was accomplished, it would split the colonies in two, isolating commercial New England from the agricultural colonies of the west and south. The Hudson also would provide a navigable inland waterway for the transportation of British troops and supplies from Canada.

The campaign to conquer the Hudson began when Gen. John

★

That's
Not
in My
American
History
Book

156

Traitor and hero
Benedict Arnold, whose
name is synonymous with
treachery, saved the
Revolution at Saratoga.
*National Archives & Records
Administration*

Burgoyne came down out of Canada with 8,300 troops—including British regulars, German Hessians, and Indian allies. His objective was to defeat the Continental Army occupying the region and capture Albany, New York. To support Burgoyne, a British force of some 1,800, led by Col. Barry St. Leger, was to attack from the west. Meanwhile, troops under Gen. Sir Henry Clinton, stationed in New York City, were to march north, forcing rebel forces to retreat before them. The British plan was to sweep the Colonials before these three armies, trap them at Albany, and destroy the Continental Army there in a three-pronged attack.

To face Burgoyne and meet the British challenge, the Continental Congress inexplicably chose Gen. Horatio Gates to command the Colonial Army occupying the Hudson River Valley. Gates replaced Maj. Gen. Philip Schuyler, who had proven himself a capable field commander but could not get along with the Congress. By contrast, Gates was a boorish windbag with little military experience and even less imagination. But he was a darling of the Congress.

To face the British, Gates had some 14,000 ill-trained and poorly organized troops scattered around him, and not a clue what he should do with them. That is when Gen. Benedict Arnold arrived on the scene to save him. Arnold knew what to do. He was, without doubt, America's most talented field commander. With only a small force, Arnold had taken the war to Canada and

Arnold's temptation
Peggy Shippen, the 18-year-old daughter of a British Loyalist, led Benedict Arnold to betray his country.
Dictionary of American Portraits

placed Quebec City under siege. Although the Colonial invasion of Canada fell short of victory, it did serve to tie up British forces north of the border for an extended period of time. Forced by superior numbers to retreat back to the colonies, Arnold had been assigned to support Gates at Saratoga.

The first thing Arnold did was to eliminate the threat of an attack from the west. With only 1,000 men, he bluffed St. Leger's British force into abandoning Fort Stanwix and retreating back to Canada, cutting off one of the three potential prongs of attack.

Upon arriving at Saratoga, Arnold was dismayed to find the Continental soldiers sitting, inactive, in ill-organized defensive positions with Buryogne poised to attack them. Arnold was especially upset to find the Continental Army's left flank fully exposed and the supine Gates unwilling to do anything about it. And on September 19, 1777, that is precisely where Burgoyne struck.

Arnold pleaded with Gates to release troops to him to meet the attack. Gates, incapable of making a forceful decision, finally released a small force to Arnold, who sent it against the British advance at Freeman's Farm. When it appeared his outmanned Colonials would be pushed back, Arnold defied Gates's orders and brought additional troops into the action. Following a bloody four-hour struggle, the British assault was haulted. Although Burgoyne held the field, the British invasion force had suffered heavy casualties.

⭐

**That's
Not
in My
American
History
Book**

As stated earlier, Saratoga was not a single battle but a series of battles fought over a period of several weeks. In each instance it was Arnold who met the enemy and prevailed. As the battles raged, Gates refused to leave what he perceived to be the safety of his camp, heavily fortified with troops he refused to release for combat. During the critical Battle of Bemis Heights, Gates sat in his tent, discussing the merits of the American rebellion with a captured British officer while Arnold slugged it out with Burgoyne.

Burgoyne's reinforcements never arrived from New York. General Clinton and his troops could not fight their way through local militias to get to Saratoga. With Burgoyne's force short of rations and having been repulsed at every turn, the general ordered a retreat back to Canada. The order came too late. By then, Arnold had circled behind the British Army and cut off its escape. Burgoyne was left with no choice but to surrender some 5,000 men.

Two important events occurred as a result of Arnold's brilliant victory at Saratoga: France signed a secret alliance with the colonies and provided funds, weapons, warships, and troops, without which the Americans could not have won the war. And the Continental Congress proclaimed Horatio Gates "The hero of Saratoga."

Arnold received two wounds at Saratoga, one to his left leg and the other to his rather enormous ego. Arnold's disaffection with the Continental Congress did not begin with Saratoga. For some time he had been battling the politicians with the same stubbornness he had exhibited while fighting the British. Arnold had been passed over for promotion and had brooded when others received credit for victories he had won. At one point he had resigned from the army in disgust, only to have George Washington talk him into changing his mind.

Meanwhile, the career of the sublimely incompetent Gates was on the rise. The Continental Congress even considered turning over Washington's command to "The Hero of Saratoga." Instead, they elevated Gates to near equal status with Washington and placed him in charge of all southern forces. It was in that capacity that the true level of Gates's incompetence finally was revealed. Upon assuming his new command, Gates requested that some of Washington's troops be transferred to his command. The doting Congress readily agreed, depleting Washington's ranks of some of his most experienced soldiers. Unfortunately, Gates did not have Arnold with him when he came up against British general Lord

Cornwallis at Camden, South Carolina. Gates suffered a defeat so humiliating that even his congressional friends were compelled to relieve him of command.

Following Saratoga, Arnold went to Philadelphia to recover from his wound. With George Washington pleading his case to the Congress, Arnold finally was given his promotion to major general. But then, like a knife thrust following a pat on the back, he was denied his seniority, leaving him ranked below officers far less competent and less deserving than himself. The final blow to Arnold's pride came when he was assigned command of the fort at West Point. In effect, the politicians had relegated their most brilliant battlefield officer to barracks duty.

While recovering in Philadelphia, Arnold became enamored with a beautiful 18-year-old girl named Peggy Shippen. She was the daughter of a British loyalist, and there is little doubt she played a role in his decision to defect to the British. Through Shippen's father, Arnold was put in touch with General Clinton who devised a scheme whereby Arnold would turn over West Point to the British. He was to be paid the equivalent of $100,000 for his betrayal. The plot was discovered when Continental soldiers captured a courier carrying plans for the takeover, and Arnold was forced to flee to avoid capture.

The British made him a brigadier general and gave him command of a poorly organized unit composed mostly of Tories and deserters. Arnold quickly demonstrated his abilities by using them to capture Richmond, Virginia. He won several engagements before marching north to besiege New London, Connecticut. If Arnold had been given a disciplined army, there is every likelihood he might have turned the tide of the conflict back in favor of the British.

Three years after Arnold's defection, a combined force of 8,000 French troops and 7,000 Colonials trapped and defeated Cornwallis's army at Yorktown, effectively ending the war. As the battle raged, the French Navy patrolled the coastline, cutting off British reinforcements and assuring victory. Ironically, without Arnold, the French would not have been at Yorktown were it not for Arnold's performance at Saratoga. In fact, there would not have been a Yorktown, because the war would have been lost years before.

With the surrender of General Cornwallis, Arnold and Shippen escaped to England. His reception there was hardly what he

★

That's
Not
in My
American
History
Book

160

expected. Arnold discovered the British despised him almost as much as his fellow Americans. Arnold received some $35,000 over the years, most of it in the form of a pension, but he never received the $100,000 he was promised.

In recent years, attempts have been made to clear Arnold's name. Supporters have gone so far as to suggest he was framed, forcing him to defect to the British. There is little credible evidence to support such a claim.

It should be noted that the American Revolution produced a different kind of war, one in which defections were commonplace. As the tide of events shifted, so did sentiments. Tories joined the Colonial armies, and Colonials joined the British. Loyalty often depended on who happened to be winning at the time. Seldom mentioned in history texts is that during the bitter cold winter of 1778, some 2,000 Continental soldiers deserted, and most of them made their way to Philadelphia to sign up with General Howe's British Army. Although the actions of others hardly justify Arnold's betrayal, it does illustrate that loyalty was a rather fleeting commodity during that war.

At Saratoga today there stands an unusual monument. It has no human face or even a name on it. It is a bas-relief depicting a cannon, a wreath, a major general's epaulet, and a left-foot military boot. The monument is a wordless tribute to Benedict Arnold and his victory in one of the most important battles in the history of humankind.

Andrew Jackson Dodges A Bullet

Andrew Jackson spent a lifetime fighting foes, ranging from Indians in the Georgia wilderness to bankers with lace cuffs at the Bank of America. He fought in barroom brawls and pistol duels. He fought the British at New Orleans, and even threatened to send U.S. troops to invade South Carolina. He faced death many times and managed to elude it. Ironically, he would come closest to a violent death not on a field of battle or in a duel at dawn, but in the relative safety of the rotunda of the Capitol building in Washington, D.C.

There on the morning of January 30, 1835, Jackson escaped an assassination attempt in an incident that would have a profound effect on the nation's criminal justice system. It was the first known attempt to assassinate a president of the United States.

Jackson, then sixty-eight, was in his second term as president when, in the company of several of his aides, he went to the House of Representatives to attend a memorial service for Warren Davis of South Carolina. The service completed, the old soldier-statesman strolled out into the Capitol rotunda, a caped greatcoat swinging from his shoulders and a walking stick in his hand. He walked several steps ahead of his companions, as was his custom.

Without warning, a young man quickly approached the president, seeming to appear out of nowhere. He was neat in dress and appearance, except for a rather heavy beard that was out of fashion for the time. In the light of the rotunda there was a glint as he raised his hand, and Jackson found himself staring into the barrel of a pistol not six feet away. The explosion that followed was deafening in the confines of the place.

Those who witnessed it were stunned by the quickness with which the event had taken place. The assassin was equally stunned when the president did not fall. The gun had misfired, exploding the detonating cap while leaving the deadly ball in its chamber.

Although everyone around Jackson seemed frozen, the old

That's
Not
in My
American
History
Book

162

soldier moved quickly toward his assailant, instinctively swinging his cane as he advanced. The young man backed away, drew a second pistol, and pulled the trigger. There was another explosion and still Jackson was standing. Just like the first pistol, the second one also had misfired.

Jackson clubbed the man with his cane, and several aides rushed forward to wrestle him to the floor.

When the guns were examined, both were found to be in excellent condition and, by all appearances, they seemed to have been properly loaded. Why they did not fire was a mystery. The chance of both misfiring under such circumstances was incalculable.

The man who attempted to kill the president was Richard Lawrence, a young Englishman who obviously was mentally deranged. Under questioning, he stated that he was the rightful heir to the throne of England and blamed President Jackson for preventing him from claiming the crown.

Old Hickory escapes
Andrew Jackson faced down an assassin in the Capitol rotunda.
Metropolitan Museum of Art, Dick Fund

When Lawrence went to trial, the Washington, D.C., jury in his case stunned the nation with its decision. The jurors found that Lawrence was not responsible for his actions by reason of insanity and sentenced him to confinement for life in an asylum. The disposition of the case unleashed a storm of controversy. Never before had a case been disposed of in such a manner. Did insanity excuse a person from punishment for their crime? Was it justice to hang a man who obviously was mad? It was the first time such questions had been widely debated.

In the wake of the verdict, it generally was agreed that anyone found guilty of attempting to assassinate the president should be hanged whether sane or insane. Among those who believed that was the attorney general for the District of Columbia, who prosecuted the case.

The prosecutor argued passionately that an attack on the president was an attack on the nation itself, and the guilty party deserved the most severe penalty possible. To his great disappointment, the jury rejected his argument.

With the passage of years, the story of the attempt on President Jackson's life has faded into forgotten history. But the court case still casts a long legal shadow every time a plea of innocent by reason of insanity is entered in an American courtroom.

As for the prosecutor who argued his case with such determination, only to lose? None other than Francis Scott Key, the man who wrote the words to "The Star-Spangled Banner."

We all know about Benjamin Franklin. Not only was he one of the nation's founding fathers, he was an inventor, foreign diplomat, publisher, and early experimenter with electricity. But did you know he only went to the second grade? Or did you realize that, in spite of his limited exposure to traditional education, he accomplished the following:

- ☞ Invented the catheter still used in hospitals today
- ☞ Invented bifocal glasses
- ☞ Printed the first mail order catalog
- ☞ Established the nation's first insurance company
- ☞ Helped set up the first subscription library
- ☞ Invented the lightning rod
- ☞ Invented a heater, the Franklin Stove, still in use today
- ☞ Organized the first volunteer fire department
- ☞ Helped organize the academy that became the University of Pennsylvania
- ☞ Reinvented the harmonica as a parlor instrument popular in Europe
- ☞ First demonstrated that acidic soils can be made fertile by adding lime
- ☞ Did much to develop the science of electricity and give it a vocabulary
- ☞ Completed noteworthy research in science and medicine

The list does not end there.

Franklin was America's first international celebrity. As a foreign diplomat, he was the toast of European society, a "must invite" to social functions during his assignments in Paris and London. Equally relaxed in the presence of royalty or lifting mugs with row-

Renaissance man Benjamin Franklin achieved numerous distinctions as an inventor, writer, and statesman. *National Archives & Records Administration*

dies at the local tavern, he also lived with the Iroquois Indians in order to study their form of democratic government.

His accomplishments are mind-boggling, and are made even more so considering his humble beginnings. Franklin was the tenth of seventeen children in a family of little means. He became a printer's apprentice, a printer, and then a publisher, and retired at age forty-one, independently wealthy.

To his neighbors, young Ben Franklin was a strange one, indeed. What else could be said of a man who would attempt to fly kites in lightning storms? And what manner of madman would try to electrocute a turkey at a picnic, using something called electricity, almost killing himself in the process?

Actually, Franklin's fascination for kites and electricity began at an early age. As a small boy he built a huge kite with enough pull to tug a boat across a pond. Upon reaching adulthood, his quenchless, childlike curiosity made him an inventor without peer in his time. When he noticed that most of the heat from fireplaces went up the chimney, he designed the Franklin Stove. The design is still practical and the stove is still in use. When his brother had a gall bladder operation, Franklin invented the catheter, also still used today.

Franklin was interested in electricity from his youth, but a friend named Peter Collinson was responsible for turning curiosity into obsession. Collison gave him a glass rod from London that gave off sparks of static electricity when rubbed, and Franklin spent a lifetime trying to find out why. In the process he helped pioneer the science of electricity and give it a vocabulary. It was Franklin who coined the words *armature, battery, charge, condenser, conductor, discharge*, and others.

166

Not all of Franklin's experiments were successful. During his attempt to electrocute a turkey at a picnic, he accidentally touched two wires and received a jolt that almost rendered him unconscious. Exhibiting his ever-present wit, he joked about the incident, comparing himself to a dolt who would try to measure the contents of a keg of gunpowder with a red-hot poker. History does not explain why Franklin decided to electrocute a turkey instead of employing more traditional methods of execution.

True to his nature as a prankster, he constructed a small metal crown which he placed atop a replica of the hated King George III of England. He devised a gadget to shock anyone who touched it. Franklin delighted in urging unwary visitors to touch the crown.

Among Franklin's other achievements:

He discovered that diseases spread more rapidly in poorly ventilated rooms, which defied prevailing medical logic at the time. He was the first to conduct a scientific study of the movement of the Gulf Stream in the Atlantic Ocean. He charted its speed, depth, and temperatures at various seasons; and his findings proved useful to naval officers, sailors, and scientists for many years. Finally, he was appointed deputy postmaster of the Colonial Postal Service with instructions to straighten out the inept institution. He not only straightened it out, he made it turn a profit.

While still a young man, Franklin began printing *Poor Richard's Almanac*. As its publisher he became a weatherman, astrologer, agricultural advisor, and internationally acclaimed wit. Many of our common sayings came from Franklin's agile mind. Among his observations:

"Three can keep a secret if two of them are dead."

"Fish and visitors begin to smell after three days."

"Keep your eyes open before marriage and half closed afterwards."

Although his publishing ventures made him a wealthy man, he was never obsessed with earning money. He never took out a single patent on any of his inventions.

Franklin also left his mark on the political world. He was a signer of the Declaration of Independence, and he negotiated with France to provide the struggling colonies with weapons, ships, troops, and financial aid, without which Americans could not have defeated Great Britain in the War for Independence. With the conclusion of the war he went to Paris and negotiated the peace. Yet, despite being an enemy of the British, he was so respected he was elected to membership in the exclusive Royal Society of London.

In a life filled with achievement, Franklin experienced one great disappointment. His campaign to have the turkey selected as the symbol of America was unsuccessful. Congress chose the eagle instead.

Despite his many accomplishments, he remained humble until the day he died. His will begins simply, "I, Benjamin Franklin of Philadelphia, printer . . ."

PART
FOUR
*From
Mutton
Head
to Slick
Willie*

167

Sports and the Presidency

Recent years have witnessed a continuing debate over the value of sports on the nation's school campuses. Academics question whether competitive sports are of any real benefit in the development of the nation's youth. Those who support athletics on campus argue that the discipline and competitiveness inherent in sports help prepare young participants for achievement in life.

Among those who considered sports a waste of time was Thomas Jefferson, who wrote: "Games played with the ball ... are too violent for the body and stamp no character on the mind." Yet in spite of Jefferson's contempt for games, it can be noted that, almost to a man, our presidents have been athletes or sportsmen.

During Bill Clinton's occupancy of the White House, he was a dedicated if not accomplished golfer with an announced goal to break into the 80s. Unfortunately, when he finally announced that he had shot an 84, his credibility was such that nobody believed him.

His predecessor, George Bush, was an outstanding college athlete. He played on championship soccer and baseball teams at Yale University. Ronald Reagan played football and baseball, was an excellent swimmer, and once worked as a sports announcer. Gerald Ford turned down a pro football contract to study law. Dwight Eisenhower played on the Army football team and was a minor league baseball player. Richard Nixon played football in college and later became an obsessive bowler with an average of 152, and Jimmy Carter loved long-distance running and organizing impromptu softball games.

Of our early presidents, George Washington had a reputation as an athlete and sportsman. It was said he could throw a coin across the Potomac River. It may or may not have been true, but the fact that the story persisted indicates that young Washington was respected for his athletic prowess.

What is known to be true was Washington's passion for playing the ponies. Like most horse players, he had at least one-well known eccentricity. If there was a gray horse in the field, he would bet on it. Washington had his own stable of race horses, and at one time owned forty-nine brood mares. When his horses ran, he bet heavily on them and was a frequent winner.

So fierce was Washington's competitive nature that when the stewards at Alexandria, Virginia, awarded first place to a rival entry in a close race, he put up such a furious protest that the Jockey Club reversed the judges' decision. Washington's gambling instincts and stubborn combativeness no doubt served him well in dealing with the Continental Congress.

A renowned athlete of a slightly later era was John Quincy Adams. In his youth, Adams was a competitive swimmer who won many races. After he became president, he continued to take regular swims in the Potomac River, even when the waters were swift and dangerous.

Andrew Jackson, like Washington, raised and raced fine horses. In 1806, he sent his horse Truxton against another famous horse named Ploughboy in a match race at Clover Bottom, North Carolina. The crowd that showed up for the race was the largest ever assembled for a sporting event in America until that time. Truxton won and Jackson pocketed both the $3,000 purse and a $10,000 side bet.

Jackson also participated, successfully, in the most deadly of all physical competitions—the pistol duel. In 1807, he became a celebrity after a duel at Harrison Mills, Kentucky. His adversary was a famous pistol shot who had dispatched several men. His bullet wounded Jackson, but Jackson's bullet killed his opponent.

Abraham Lincoln never fought a duel, but he gained regional fame in Illinois as a wrestler. Tall and rather bony in appearance, Lincoln did not look like a wrestler, which allowed his friends to line up unwary challengers and receive good betting odds. Inevitably, Lincoln would quickly pin his opponent and win the match.

Lincoln was one of our most athletic presidents. He was described as "hard as nails" by his friends. According to one historian, "he was a good runner and swimmer, a master jumper and crowbar heaver." (The historian does not explain if crowbar heav-

PART
FOUR
*From
Mutton
Head
to Slick
Willie*

169

★

That's
Not
in My
American
History
Book

ing was a sport of the day or an act of aggression.) Lincoln also was an excellent shot with a rifle and a fine horseman. It is relatively unknown that he was one of the best handball players in Illinois. Records exist listing Lincoln as the champion of various competitions in Illinois back when the game was still known under its old English name, "the game of fives."

William McKinley was another president with a continuing interest in sports. In fact, he saved the traditional Army-Navy football game.

By 1894, the game between the military academies had degenerated into what amounted to an annual war between the teams. But that year an especially bloody brawl erupted between the cadets and midshipmen, and onlookers joined the fray. Tempers ran so high that an aged general slapped an admiral. The action resulted in a challenge to a duel. Fortunately, the participants were not very good shots and missed each other.

When President Grover Cleveland heard about the incident, he issued an executive order banning the game.

Upon taking office, President McKinley summoned the officials of both institutions to his office. He told them he thought the game should be renewed, but warned against a repeat of the events of 1894. The Army-Navy game resumed in 1899 after a ban of five years and has continued to this day as one of the nation's premier sporting events.

President Theodore Roosevelt was an exceptional athlete. Ironically, as a youth, he was frail and so nearsighted he could see no more than ten feet without his glasses. Still he persisted in playing various sports and in the process suffered a broken arm, broken nose, broken ribs, and a fractured leg.

True to his stubborn nature, Roosevelt built himself into an imposing physical specimen. He learned how to box. He became an expert horseman. Following the death of his wife in New York, he went west, started a ranch, and became a working cowboy. When a burly cowboy in a frontier bar tried to provoke a fight with him, Roosevelt knocked him cold with one punch, earning the respect of his western peers. He became a deputy sheriff and tracked down and captured a gang of cattle rustlers. Later, after becoming president, he sometimes invited famous boxers to the White House to spar with him. One such session became so heated, Roosevelt sustained a blow that cost him the sight in one eye.

Roosevelt was a big game hunter who stood his ground to bring down charging rhinos, water buffalo, and grizzly bears. To over-

★

PART
FOUR
*From
Mutton
Head
to Slick
Willie*

Rough 'n' Ready Teddy
Theodore Roosevelt,
one-time Dakota rancher
and deputy sheriff,
captured a band of cattle
rustlers.
*Historical Society of North
Dakota*

come his fear of heights, he became a mountain climber, scaling both the Matterhorn and Jungfrau. His physical stamina and determination were illustrated in an incident that occurred in 1912. While making a speech, he was shot in the chest in an assassination attempt. As police hauled away the madman who pulled the trigger, Roosevelt stubbornly returned to the podium to complete his speech before collapsing from loss of blood.

Every football fan owes Teddy Roosevelt a debt of gratitude. He saved the game. In 1905, there was a frightful toll of human life on the gridiron. Across the nation, no less than thirty-two players were killed in football games. The nation's press demanded the game be abolished. Preachers railed against football from their pulpits. College presidents forbid their students to play the game, and thirty state legislatures introduced bills to make it illegal to play football. But Roosevelt thought the game worth saving.

He called a conference of leading college officials and urged them not to outlaw the game, but to improve it and make it safe to play. Under his guidance an organization to govern the game was formed and rules instituted to eliminate the rough play that

★

That's
Not
in My
American
History
Book

plagued the game. As a result of that conference, football has risen beyond mere sport to become a part of American culture. The organization Roosevelt helped create was the National Collegiate Athletic Association (NCAA), which still governs collegiate athletics.

Another president who made a significant contribution to the game of football was Woodrow Wilson. As a lad Wilson wanted to be a baseball player, but because he was nearsighted, he could never excel at the game. Upon entering Princeton University, he went out for the baseball team but failed to make the squad. He then turned to coaching, at which he was very successful.

Recognizing his leadership qualities, Princeton officials hired him to coach the football team. He proved to be a football wizard and, in fact, left his mark on the modern game. Before Wilson came on the scene, football plays were simple. Formations were crudely organized, and power was the most important factor in the game. He was the first to draw up intricate plays utilizing blocking angles, fakes, traps, and reverses. He taught blocking and tackling techniques that allowed quickness to overcome brute strength and made deception an important part of the game. Some of the basics he taught are still fundamental to the game today.

Wilson's innovations and leadership produced a mighty Princeton team. Unlike other coaches, he never gave fiery pep talks but quietly lectured his players on honor, decency, teamwork, and sportsmanship—qualities that would serve him well in the White House.

Franklin Roosevelt was another athlete who became president. Long before he achieved a record of four terms in the White House, he set a track and field record that remains unbroken to this day. Before being crippled by polio, Roosevelt set a national high school record for the standing high jump. The event later was eliminated from track and field competition and, as a result, the record still stands.

Dwight Eisenhower had the distinction of being the only U.S. president to tackle the legendary Jim Thorpe. It turned out to be a dubious distinction because, in doing so, he also became the only president to have his leg broken by Jim Thorpe. It happened November 9, 1912 when a powerful Carlisle College team, led by Thorpe, played Army. Eisenhower had to be carried from the field. The broken leg ended his football career at West Point. Carlisle won the game 27–6.

Eisenhower also was an outstanding baseball player, who might

**PART
FOUR**
*From
Mutton
Head
to Slick
Willie*

173

Ike at the bat
Dwight Eisenhower
played under an
assumed name for a
Kansas minor league
baseball team.
*National Archives &
Records Administration*

have made it to the major leagues had he pursued the game as a career. He played minor league baseball for Junction City in the Central Kansas League under the name of "Wilson" back in 1911. The use of assumed names was common among college athletes who wanted to pick up a few dollars playing professional baseball in the summer while protecting their amateur standing for collegiate sports.

But "Wilson" was so good that area sportswriters began writing glowing articles about him. That attracted major league scouts to the park to check out the "Wilson" kid, but to Eisenhower, baseball was only a summer diversion. His real ambition was to play football at West Point that autumn. Rather than risk his amateur standing, he quit the baseball team and quietly left town.

President John F. Kennedy's athletic endeavors were limited by a back injury when he occupied the White House. However, as a young man, he played all of the usual sports young men play. He was a good tennis player, loved swimming and sailing, and delighted in organizing touch football games for friends and family. He was a fiery competitor who would go to almost any length to win even the most innocent game.

When Richard Nixon became president, one of the first things

That's
Not
in My
American
History
Book

he did was instruct workmen to cover an indoor swimming pool and install a bowling lane over it. Nixon approached bowling like he did everything else—obsessively. He often could be found late at night, wearing a shirt and necktie, bowling by himself on his private lane. Nixon had Secret Service agents keep meticulous records. His average was 152. His high game was 232.

Nixon was a rabid football fan. Recalling his days as a substitute lineman at Whittier College in California, teammates said that when Nixon finally got in a game he was so eager to play that he frequently jumped offside—a habit he could not seem to overcome once he became president. While in the White House, he became a fan of the Washington Redskins. He even found time to draw up plays for the Redskins, which he sent to Coach George Allen. It is not known if Coach Allen ever used any of these presidential plays in a game.

Gerald Ford was an outstanding athlete. Unfortunately, once he became president, he earned a reputation for being something of a klutz when he stumbled down an airplane ramp in front of the cameras of the Washington press corps. It also did not help his image as an athlete when TV cameras showed him bouncing a golf ball off of a spectator at a celebrity tournament. Unknown to most of the press at the time was that Ford's occasional awkwardness was the result of an old knee injury from his football playing days.

As a schoolboy, Ford captained his high school football team at Grand Rapids, Michigan. He earned numerous awards and attracted the attention of college scouts, finally signing with the University of Michigan and becoming an all-star lineman for the Wolverines. He was offered contracts by the Detroit Lions and Chicago Bears, but turned them down to become a coach at Yale and pursue a law degree.

Secret Service agents assigned to President Jimmy Carter had to be in good physical condition. He loved to hunt and fish, and was a dedicated runner who occasionally entered long-distance races, requiring his agents to run along beside him. Carter also delighted in organizing softball games between the press corps that followed him around and his own aides and Secret Service agents.

Ronald Reagan was a devoted athlete throughout his youth and a rabid sports fan during his tenure in the White House. He was a football lineman in high school and college. He also worked as a lifeguard while attending Eureka College in Illinois. He later

The First Golfer
"Jumbo Bill" Taft
launches a putt.
Culver Collection

PART
FOUR
*From
Mutton
Head
to Slick
Willie*

175

landed a job as a sports announcer for a radio station in Des Moines, Iowa.

However, Reagan's greatest claim to athletic fame was a result of movie magic rather than personal achievement on the gridiron. He became famous for his screen portrayal of legendary football player George Gipp. So closely did he become associated with the movie character that more than a half-century later, his friends were still calling him "The Gipper."

George Bush was an avid athlete who became president. While in the White House he still found time for tennis, horseshoes, table tennis, jogging, hunting, and fishing. He also enjoyed impromptu softball and touch football games.

At Yale, Bush played soccer on a team that won the New England championship and was first baseman and captain on a Yale baseball squad that was among the top college teams in the nation. In 1947 and 1948, Bush helped lead his team to the finals of the national championship series before being defeated. He was considered a good fielder but only an adequate hitter, batting .264 his senior year.

If there is a true presidential sport, it must be golf. Almost all of

That's

Not

in My

American

History

Book

our modern-day presidents have played the game, from William Howard Taft to Bill Clinton.

If not the best presidential golfer, Dwight Eisenhower was the most persistent. His dedication to the sport was rewarded in 1954 when the Golf Writers of America voted him the Outstanding Golfer of the Year.

Several other golfing presidents would have given Eisenhower a good game. One of them was Warren G. Harding, who often played against famed pro Chick Evans and consistently shot in the 80s. He was so obsessed with the game and spent so much time on the links his cabinet became known as the "Golf Cabinet."

Another outstanding player was the 300-pound Taft. He trained for the rigors of his election campaigns by walking the fairways. It was Taft who introduced golf terminology into politics. He peppered his speeches with words like "stymied," "in the rough," and "bunkered."

On one occasion, Taft was made a member of a Boston country club for the purpose of inviting him to participate in its annual golf tournament. It was intended as an honorary gesture only. But to the astonishment of club members, Taft won the tournament, pocketed the $1,000 prize, thanked the organizers, and departed for Washington.

Did sports help these men attain their lofty political goals, or did their inherent competitiveness naturally attract them to sports? One thing is clear. An inordinate number of our presidents won distinction on the playing fields long before they did so in the political arena.

The Remarkable Luck of FDR

It was a typical Washington, D.C., party. As it came to a close, it became obvious that several of the guests had visited the champagne fountain too often, including the attorney general of the United States, who was looking for a ride home. He approached a young acquaintance to ask if he would give him a lift, and the young man agreed.

The year was 1919, and the attorney general was one of the most famous and controversial men in America at the time. Mitchell Palmer had earned his celebrity in a well-publicized campaign to rid the nation of Communists, anarchists, and terrorists. His heavy-handed, often illegal methods in pursuit of that goal had drawn sharp criticism from the nation's newspapers, but Palmer was adored by the masses. In fact, he was so popular he was being touted as a possible presidential candidate.

The young man who agreed to give Palmer a ride that night was the assistant secretary of the Navy. Upon his arrival at the Palmer residence, he parked in the driveway, and the two men engaged in conversation for several minutes. Palmer kept insisting that the driver join him in his library for a nightcap. The young man continued to graciously decline the offer, pointing out that it was very late and he faced a busy day in the morning. Finally, Palmer thanked him and watched him drive away.

Upon entering his house, Palmer stopped briefly in the library before going upstairs. He was preparing to retire for the night when a massive explosion shook the house. Palmer rushed downstairs to find the front of his house blown away. Part of the front wall was lying in the library where he had been only minutes before. As a result of his zeal to rid the nation of terrorists, Palmer himself had become a target of terrorism. Observing the destruction in the library, he realized that if the young man who gave him

⭐

**That's
Not
in My
American
History
Book**

the ride had accepted his invitation for a nightcap, both would be dead.

Mitchell Palmer never became president, but the young man who declined the invitation for a nightcap did—four times. His name was Franklin D. Roosevelt.

From that day until his death at Warm Springs, Georgia, twenty-six years later, Roosevelt would lead a paradoxical existence. He would live in a world of leg braces, canes, and wheelchairs. Yet, he would lead what seemed a charmed existence, because he would brush shoulders with death four times and escape.

Following his escape in the bombing of Mitchell Palmer's home, Roosevelt's next brush with death came just two years later. It began on an August morning in 1921, at his summer home on Campobello Island, just off the coast of Maine. When Roosevelt tried to get out of bed, he sensed something was dreadfully wrong. His left leg was not working properly. As he exited the bed, he fell. It seemed that, overnight, the leg had become useless to him. Doctors informed him that he had been stricken with a viral infection called poliomyelitis—more commonly known as polio.

Roosevelt had gone swimming the previous afternoon and developed a chill. He went to bed early, thinking his discomfort was nothing more than a bad cold. He had gone to bed a robust, athletic man in his late thirties and awakened with polio, fighting for his life.

Soon Roosevelt lost the feeling in his right leg and then in the lower half of his body. His mother, wife, and doctors urged him to retire to the family estate at Hyde Park where he could be properly cared for. But Roosevelt was determined not to become permanently immobilized. With persistence, he taught himself to walk with canes and metal leg braces. Ever a politician at heart, he announced his candidacy for the New York governorship, and won. He then ran for president, received the Democratic Party nomination, and won the election by defeating Herbert Hoover in the fall of 1932.

On February 15, just three weeks before his inauguration, Roosevelt was in Miami, Florida, to deliver a speech. As a large crowd welcomed the president-elect and accompanying dignitaries, a woman in the audience was stunned to see a man standing beside her lift a revolver and point it toward the president. She instinctively grabbed the man's arm just as the weapon fired. The bullet intended for Roosevelt struck Mayor Anton J. Cermack of Chicago.

The mayor died of his wound on March 6, just two days after Roosevelt was inaugurated as president. The gunman, a known anarchist named Joseph Zangara, was promptly tried, convicted, and executed.

The president came close to death on at least one other occasion. It happened November 14, 1943, when the world was at war. Roosevelt and his Joint Chiefs of Staff were holding a secret meeting aboard the battleship *Iowa*. As the ship with its VIP passengers plowed through the Atlantic, the crew of an American submarine patrolling the area mistakenly launched a torpedo. To the crewmen's horror, the torpedo seemed to be heading straight for the *Iowa*. Luckily, it cut across the wake of the ship, barely missing it. The crew was relieved that they had not accidentally destroyed a battleship, little realizing how close they came to perhaps killing the President of the United States as well as the Joint Chiefs of Staff.

Death finally overtook the president in 1945 at his vacation retreat at Warm Springs. It was there Franklin Roosevelt died quietly in bed of a brain hemorrhage. The man whose family and friends had urged to resign himself to life as a permanent invalid in 1921 had been elected president of the United States four times. He had

PART
FOUR
*From
Mutton
Head
to Slick
Willie*

179

The indestructible Executive Franklin Delano Roosevelt, here meeting with Winston Churchill and Joseph Stalin, survived several brushes with death. *National Archives & Records Administration*

**That's
Not
in My
American
History
Book**

forever altered the course of the nation's government, creating social programs that would be copied by nations around the world. And he had led his country out of the Great Depression and guided it to victory in the greatest war in the history of humankind.

General Putnam under the Knife

 He was short, homely, usually a little disheveled, and a bit overweight. He had only a limited education and little interest in politics or religion. He was humble and unassuming, rarely initiating a conversation, and his stoic expression seldom betrayed his emotions. But Israel Putnam ranks right up there with America's most colorful military heroes.

When British troops advanced on Bunker Hill, he was the colonial officer who told his men: "Don't fire until you see the whites of their eyes." But his military career also was marked by another, more dubious distinction. Israel Putnam is the only American general to be scalped by Indians and live to tell about it.

Putnam's reputation as a fighting man was legendary, even in his lifetime. If there was a war, or even the hint of one, he would be in the middle of it. In an off-and-on military career that spanned more than thirty years and included stints in the colonial and British armies, he probably participated in more campaigns than any of his eighteenth century contemporaries. His appearance and unassuming manner aside, Putnam seemed to live for the thunder of cannon and the smell of spent powder. He was absolutely fearless in combat and, given an order, was bound to carry it out.

He experienced his first combat in the French and Indian War. In 1755 he fought in a series of battles that halted a French invasion of New York, and he distinguished himself at the Battle of Lake George. In 1759, he was given command of a British regiment, and he participated in the British West Indies campaign in 1762. Two years later, when Detroit came under siege by Chief Pontiac and a large force of warriors, Putnam commanded the army that liberated the city.

During the French and Indian War, Putnam was badly wounded in battle. As he lay unconscious, he was set upon by

That's
Not
in My
American
History
Book

Indians who, thinking he was dead, scalped him. To the amaze-
ment of his assailants, he was discovered to be still alive. Taken
into captivity, Putnam was strapped to a stake. His captors were
preparing to burn him alive when a French officer intervened and
convinced them to spare his life.

In the spring of 1775, Putnam was plowing his fields when a
servant ran up to inform him that British and Colonial forces had
clashed at Lexington and Concord. Without saying a word, Putnam began unhitching the team. He climbed aboard one of the
horses and instructed the servant to fetch his gun and sword from
the house and to follow him on the other horse. He then went off
to war riding a plow horse, leaving the plow sitting in its furrow.

George Washington had him commissioned a general in the
Continental Army. The men placed under him at Bunker Hill
were skeptical that their commander was up to the task. He certainly did not fit the traditional image of a general: He was elderly,
somewhat pudgy, and did not appear at all ferocious. And some in
the ranks sported more impressive uniforms than their general.
But he quickly earned their respect.

Putnam was inspecting the work of the troops digging fortifica-
tions at Bunker Hill when he spotted a large stone and asked a soldier to place it on the wall. The soldier's back stiffened and he
protested.

"Sir, I am a corporal!" he pointed out.

"I ask your pardon, sir," the general said as he dismounted.
Putnam picked up the rock and placed it on the wall himself, to the
delight of the men in the ranks and the embarrassment of the corporal.

Following the battle at Bunker Hill, Washington gave Putnam
the Long Island command. Among the troops eventually placed
under him were smartly dressed and highly disciplined Hessian
soldiers. By contrast, Putnam wore a uniform of homespun cloth
because that is what the Colonials under him wore. He also ate
what they ate and slept where they slept.

To the Hessian troops from Europe under his command, Putnam did not look or act like a general and the old man became the
butt of their jokes. One soldier would write of him, "This old gray
beard might be a good, honest man but nobody but the rebels
would make him a general."

Attitudes changed when the shooting started. Putnam had seen
battles the young Hessians could not even imagine, and his cool-

ness in combat quickly won them over. After seeing Putnam under fire, that same Hessian soldier would grudgingly write of him: "He seems totally unfit for anything except fighting."

It was a tribute that, no doubt, would have made Israel Putnam proud.

Scalping survivor Gen. Israel Putnam holds the distinction of being the only general ever to have survived a scalping. *National Archives & Records Administration*

On a crisp October afternoon in Atlanta in 1916, Georgia Tech's powerful football team took the field against little Cumberland College in a grid-iron contest that rewrote the record books and became a footnote in sports history.

No one expected Cumberland to win the game. Georgia Tech had one of the most powerful teams in the nation that year. But no one anticipated the massacre that took place.

Fate had lined up against the Cumberland football team even before it reached Atlanta. With only sixteen players on its roster, the team stopped over in Nashville to recruit some "ringers" from the Vanderbilt football squad. The stop cost Cumberland three of its best players, who were stranded in Nashville when they missed the train to Atlanta.

As the game got under way, Georgia Tech's running backs scored at will. By half-time Tech had run over, through, and around Cumberland's hapless defense for 19 touchdowns and led by an unbelievable score of 126 to 0. But that was not good enough for the Georgia Tech coach. During the half-time break, he was inspired to give his team a pep talk.

"Men, we might be in front," he warned his players, "but you never know what those Cumberland players have up their sleeves."

All the Cumberland players had up their sleeves were bruises in abundance and a collective desire to get out of the stadium alive. But there was no mercy in the hearts of the Georgia Tech players. Several of them had been on the Tech baseball team that was humiliated when Cumberland upset them the previous spring. Inspired by their coach, the Tech players stormed back onto the field and ran up another 96 points in the second half. The final score was 222 to 0, a record that still stands.

By the time the Cumberland players limped off the field, Tech running backs had rolled up 528 yards rushing, 220 on kickoff re-

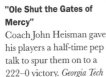

PART
FOUR
*From
Mutton
Head
to Slick
Willie*

185

"Ole Shut the Gates of Mercy"
Coach John Heisman gave his players a half-time pep talk to spur them on to a 222–0 victory. *Georgia Tech Sports Information*

turns, and another 220 on punt returns. Tech did not even throw a pass in the game.

Upon learning about the half-time pep talk when his team was leading 126 to 0, sportswriters were at least as unmerciful in their criticism of the coach as he had been in running up the score on poor Cumberland College. They labeled the Georgia Tech mentor "Ole Shut the Gates of Mercy." The name and the game would haunt him for the remainder of his coaching career. In fact, his name became synonymous with one who runs up the score on an overmatched opponent.

But in spite of his merciless reputation, the Tech coach would go on to achieve greatness and forever leave his imprint on the game. He was the man responsible for dividing football games into four quarters instead of two halves. He invented the center snap direct to the quarterback. He set up the first collegiate athletic dormitory for football players. He was the one who devised the formations that would become the "T" and the "I"—variations of which are still used by college and professional coaches.

And the Georgia Tech coach would achieve one other noteworthy distinction: In 1935, it was decided that a trophy should be awarded to the most outstanding collegiate football player in the

**That's
Not
in My
American
History
Book**

nation each year. Over the years it became one of the most prestigious individual awards in all of sports. It was called the Heisman Trophy, and it became the ultimate symbol for football excellence.

The trophy was named for John Heisman, that same Georgia Tech coach who once shut the gates of mercy on little Cumberland College.

One for the record books The scorekeeper ran out of room on the board as Georgia Tech demolished Cumberland College. *Georgia Tech Sports Information*

The Corset Maker Who Shook the World

QUESTION: Who wrote *Common Sense?*
ANSWER: Thomas Paine.
Every history student has been asked that standard test question. Regretfully, that is all most students learn about Thomas Paine. No figure in American history has been more undeservedly ignored in our textbooks, a terrible oversight because Thomas Paine was one of our nation's most colorful icons. He was an incredible rabble-rouser who shook the world with his words.

Not only did Paine light the spark that inflamed America in a revolution, he was instrumental in starting the French Revolution and even attempted to bring down the English monarchy. He was a political troublemaker without peer, whose writings gave birth to modern democracy. Yet, today he is barely remembered in the nation he helped create with the force of his rhetoric.

The reason for Paine's maltreatment by history is understandable, if not forgivable. His enemies accused him of leading an unChristian life (which was true) and of being an atheist (Paine considered himself an agnostic). He frequented taverns and drank to excess. As a result, our early historians tended to downplay his role in the tumultuous political upheavals of his time, their justification being that no one of such unsavory character should be elevated to the status of American hero.

Thomas Paine was born on January 29, 1737 in Thetford, England, a small town just north of London. His father, a devout Quaker, was the town's corset maker, and Thomas learned the craft while still a child. His rebellious nature manifested itself early. Still in his teens, he turned his back on his father's shop and ran away to become a sailor.

His youthful thirst for adventure quenched at sea, he returned home, married his childhood sweetheart, and settled down. He moved to Sandwich, England, and with borrowed money, opened

★

That's
Not
in My
American
History
Book

a corset shop. He was happy there and might have lived out his years as a contented businessman if not for a devastating event in his life. His wife died when he was in his early twenties. Her death plunged him into a state of deep depression that would last for years. He began to drink heavily and soon closed the corset shop, "disgusted with all of the toil and little gain."

Paine got a job as an excise tax collector, but he was not cut out to be a bureaucrat. His inherent rebellious nature soon got him fired. He became a teacher but did not like the confinement of the job. He had a religious reawakening and became a preacher, but soon backslid from the calling. He married for a second time, but that union turned out to be a disaster. He tried tax collecting once more and was fired following a personality clash with a superior. That incident left him burning with a hatred for bureaucracy in general and the British government and its monarchy in particular.

At that stage of his life, the only thing Paine was good at was drinking at a grog shop named the White Hart Tavern and loudly expressing his political views. He despised King George III and railed against the monarchy, contending that no man had a "divine right" to rule other men. He went through a period in which he passionately wrote poetry, which no one cared to purchase. His life changed the day a candidate for Parliament offered him three guineas to write a campaign song. The song was a success, and soon he was writing inflammatory speeches for politicians. That is when Thomas Paine found his niche in life.

At about this time Paine became acquainted with someone who would alter the course of his life once more. He met Benjamin Franklin, who was serving as an envoy to London from Colonial America. Franklin was impressed by the firebrand whose ideas on democratic government paralleled his own. He encouraged Paine to go to America, where a revolution was brewing. In the fall of 1774, Paine took his advice.

Arriving in America, Paine indeed found a revolution brewing, but it was not his kind of revolution. Colonial leaders were seeking equality with British citizens—not independence. Paine became the first to inject that forbidden word into the American mindset—independence!

The initial vehicle for Paine's revolutionary rhetoric was *Pennsylvania Magazine*, which he edited. Then, in January of 1776, he produced a pamphlet titled *Common Sense*. Because of its treasonous content, it was signed simply, "An Englishman." It caused a sensation.

His words changed the world
Thomas Paine galvanized
colonists' sentiments with his
masterful rhetoric.
*National Archives & Records
Administration*

★

PART
FOUR
*From
Mutton
Head
to Slick
Willie*

189

King George III was livid when he read it. He accused Benjamin Franklin of being the author. British authorities in America were convinced that John Adams had written it. But Thomas Jefferson knew the author. "Thomas Paine is the only other writer in America (besides himself) who could have written it," Jefferson told those who tried to credit *Common Sense* to him.

Common Sense declared in public what even the most radical of rebels dared not say aloud: The King of England was a hopeless tyrant, and the only path left open for the colonies was total independence from his clutches.

"You may as well assert that because a child has thrived on milk that it is never to have meat," Paine wrote. "The blood of the slain, the weeping voice of nature cries, 'Tis time to part!' . . . Nothing can settle our affairs so expeditiously as an open and determined declaration of independence."

Common Sense inspired Americans not only to think independence, but to shout it. The leaders of the various colonies, who could hardly agree on anything, suddenly found themselves united on the issue of independence in that momentous summer of 1776.

Common Sense sold for two shillings per copy, and it made Thomas Paine a wealthy man. Until that time no pamphlet had sold so many copies, not only in America, but across Europe as well. In England, where its circulation was prohibited, black market copies sold for astronomical prices. When the Queen caught

⭐

That's
Not
in My
American
History
Book

the Prince of Wales with a copy, he refused to tell where he got it and a scandal ensued. Just six months after *Common Sense* was published, the Continental Congress, meeting in Philadelphia, approved a Declaration of Independence, setting in motion a war with England.

In 1787, with Great Britain resigned to defeat and the colonies building a new democratic nation, Paine returned to England. He had designed a unique "pierless bridge," which he was convinced would revolutionize bridge building. Trying to convince government engineers of the worthiness of his invention, he ran head-on into the British bureaucracy once more. True to his nature, he reacted by spewing forth literature intended to incite the British to overthrow their monarchy and establish a democracy. The government reacted by having Paine indicted for treason. Before he could be arrested, he fled to France, which was bad news for the French monarchy.

In Paris, Paine began turning out pamphlets urging the French masses to rise up and fight for a democratic government. On July 1, 1791, he led the placarding of Paris, calling on the people to overthrow the monarchy.

Although the French Revolution was a success, what followed appalled Paine. He opposed the systematic executions of members of the nobility. He urged the leaders of the rebellion to exile King Louis XVI instead of executing him. The leaders proceeded to kill the king and toss Paine in jail. Upon his release from prison, he returned to America—now the United States of America. In 1809, at age seventy-two, Paine died, quietly, in New York. Ten years later, his remains were returned to England to rest in the soil of his native land.

During his turbulent lifetime, Thomas Paine had been instrumental in changing the governmental system of one nation and inspiring the birth of modern democracy in another. Although unsuccessful in convincing his fellow Englishmen to overthrow the King of England in favor of democracy, Paine's writings are credited with inspiring the Reform Bill of 1832. The bill reduced the influence of the king over British citizens and placed more governmental control in the hands of elected officials.

Throughout his life, Paine's private existence was as trouble-plagued as his public life. He never fully recovered from the loss of his first wife. His second marriage was strange indeed. From the day of the wedding, he reportedly never slept with his second wife and had little to do with her. However, despite his slight build and rather homely appearance, he had a reputation for being a ladies' man. He also had a reputation for consuming rum in excess. His critics frequently pointed to that fact when they were at a loss to argue with the ideas set forth in his writings.

The list of notable works that flowed from his pen include *Prospects on the Rubicon, Agrarian Justice, Addresses to the Addressers* and *Rights of Man.*

Although historians denied Thomas Paine his rightful place in history, none can deny his impact on today's world. He did far more than simply cost King George III thirteen American colonies. He proved that one man's pen had greater might than all the swords of France and England. For two-and-a-quarter centuries, his ideas have toppled tyrants, dictators, and kings, and the democracy that Thomas Paine once envisioned for America has become the ideal of free people everywhere.

PART FIVE

The Vikings, Belle Starr, and Lucky Lindy

Myths That Became History

One of the unfortunate realities of history is that when a myth refuses to die, it becomes history. Another reality is that some early chroniclers of the American story were not above spicing their writings with fiction. For example, much of the erroneous information surrounding Christopher Columbus comes from a three-volume biography written in the 1820s by Washington Irving. Regrettably, Irving's fiction would be repeated by generations of historians, even until today. It was Irving who made up the story that Columbus sailed west to prove the Earth was round instead of flat.

Mason Weems's cherry tree yarn, included in his biography of George Washington, is an example of a harmless bit of fiction that, somehow, became mythical history. Before the emergence of modern communication, we were a nation of storytellers. Stories were retold and embellished until they became accepted as fact. From the freedom inherent in that incubator of creative expression came many of our legends and myths. Following are a few that live on in history.

Wild West Cowboys and Outlaw Queens

 No historical era has been more compromised by fiction than the so-called wild, wild west.

In fact, the wildest thing about the American West might have been the imaginations of writers like Ned Buntline, Alton B. Meyers, and Edward L. Wheeler and editors like Richard K. Fox of the *National Police Gazette*. They and others like them cranked out countless reams of fictionalized adventure stories under the guise of truth. In doing so, they immortalized such colorful characters as Wild Bill Hickok, Buffalo Bill Cody, Calamity Jane, Billy the Kid, Deadwood Dick, Butch Cassidy and the Sundance Kid, and—lest we forget—Belle Starr, the Outlaw Queen.

The true story of Belle Starr provides a textbook example of how a Wild West legend was born. According to the story, she was a beautiful female Robin Hood who led a band of desperate outlaws. The true story is somewhat less dramatic:

Her name was Myra Belle Shirley. She was less than five feet tall and weighed ninety pounds. She had a narrow, pinched face, an oversize nose, and a recessed chin. She grew up on a north Texas farm and became a prostitute in Dallas's red-light district. When in her mid twenties, she followed one of her boyfriends to eastern Oklahoma, only to discover that he did not want her. She ended up marrying a cattle rustler named Sam Starr.

Belle was arrested only once in her life, when she and Sam stole two milk cows from Frank West, Sam's cousin. Both were sentenced to a year in jail at Fort Smith, Arkansas. The *Fort Smith Elevator* ran a brief article on Belle's apprehension for the simple reason it was unusual for a woman to be arrested for stealing milk cows.

In her later years, Belle experienced severe mental problems—probably brought on by diseases inherited from her days as a prostitute back in Dallas. She was a well-known character in Fort

⭐

That's
Not
in My
American
History
Book

196

Smith, then the seat of law for Oklahoma's Indian territory. With a long-barrel Colt strapped to her side, she strutted the streets, proclaiming to all who would listen that she was the leader of an outlaw band.

Belle Starr died on the afternoon of February 3, 1889 after being shot in the back near her home. Although there was never an arrest, it was believed she was killed by her grown son who was so mentally deranged he sometimes was chained like an animal. Her obituary ran only four lines in the Fort Smith newspaper.

Alton B. Meyers happened to read the obituary. He was a down-on-his-luck writer, broke and stranded in Fort Smith. Fascinated by the name Belle Starr, he stopped a man on the street and asked about her. Meyers discovered that she had been a nutty old woman who thought she was an outlaw queen. That was good enough for Meyers. He promptly wired the *National Police Gazette* and was commissioned to write a story. With the promise of a cash advance, he retired to a hotel room and began to write:

> Of all the women of the Cleopatra type since the days of the Egyptian queen herself, the universe had produced none more remarkable than Belle Starr, the Bandit Queen. She was more amorous than Anthony's mistress, more relentless than Pharaoh's daughter, braver than Joan of Arc . . .

With that introduction, Belle Starr became a famous outlaw queen and took her place in history beside Cleopatra and Joan of Arc.

In reality, the wild, wild west of Alton Meyers simply never existed. The era that produced the fabled American cowboy lasted only about twenty-five years, little more than a half-step in the march of history. It began following the Civil War and, for all practical purposes, was over by 1890. Yet, no period did more to define the American character. The image of free-spirited, straight-shooting cowboys riding the open range and brave lawmen defending justice with blazing six-guns is strictly American. But truth be known, far more six-guns were fired in Hollywood movie studios in the first half of the twentieth century than in the entire cowboy era of the nineteenth century.

The wild west of legend was given birth in 1865 at Appomattox, Virginia. It grew out of a restless spirit imbued in a generation of young men, North and South, who had been uprooted from their homes by war. It was fueled by an insatiable demand for beef in the eastern United States immediately following the Civil War. It did not begin on the high plains but in the grassy marshlands that line the Texas Gulf Coast.

During the war, herds of wild cows proliferated in the coastal marshes of Texas. Returning soldiers found hundreds of thousands of unbranded cattle grazing there. Some enterprising Texans began rounding up those unclaimed cattle with the intention of herding them to market.

The first trail drives were from south Texas to a railhead at Sedalia, Missouri. However, it soon became apparent that there were too many problems inherent in that route, including towns along the way and too many farms to be crossed. Drovers frequently were stopped and rerouted by lawmen called out by irate farmers who did not want cattle herds trampling their crops. The dilemma was solved by an enterprising gentleman from Springfield, Illinois, named Joseph G. McCoy.

Part con man and part entrepreneurial genius, McCoy had managed to avoid military service while making a fortune as a cattle dealer during the war. When the railroad reached Abilene, Kansas, in 1867, McCoy built a large stockyard there. He then traveled to Texas to convince the herders it would be more profitable to drive their cattle through the Oklahoma Indian Territory to his pens at Abilene. In fact, it proved so profitable that McCoy and a number of Texas ranchers became extremely wealthy. A cow worth $6 down in Texas could bring as much as $30 at McCoy's Kansas stockyard, and ranchers often turned a profit of up to $30,000 on a single drive.

Within twenty years the great cattle drives ended with the extension of rail lines to the South and Southwest. But those storied drives left us a legend—that of the American cowboy as a dashing and noble knight of the plains.

If one believes Hollywood stereotypes, almost all cowboys were white Anglo Americans. Somewhat ironic is the fact that many cowboys were Native Americans. The Pawnee and Osage were highly respected by cattlemen for their herding and horse-handling skills. In fact, some ranchers used Native Americans exclusively to care for their herds.

Following the Civil War, many African-Americans left the delta farmlands of the South to seek new opportunities out west. In the Southwest, Mexican ranch hands were predominant. Many Euro-

★

That's
Not
in My
American
History
Book

198

pean immigrants were drawn westward, and it was not at all unusual to hear a night rider crooning to a restless herd in German or French.

Contrary to his oft-portrayed image, the working cowboy was not necessarily an illiterate rowdy. In his book, *Cowboy Life: Reconstructing an American Myth*, author William W. Savage Jr. describes a group of cowboys he encountered sitting around a campfire one night:

> It was ascertained by taking stock that five out of the nine had graduated from Eastern colleges, two of the five being University of Virginia graduates and every one of the remaining four having enjoyed the advantages of a common school education.

Savage summed up the job of cowboying this way: "The work was simply more tiring than heroic and more boring than romantic."

Still, it was not a bad job for a young man. For his work the cowboy was provided a bunk and board although, on occasion, the bunk might be a blanket on the ground. He was provided a horse (he usually had his own saddle) and was paid from $20 to $30 a month. Although that might seem a paltry wage by today's standards, in the 1870s and '80s, it was almost as much as a factory worker back East could make.

The cowboy also had a chance to pick up a few extra dollars. On long cattle drives he might be paid a bonus, depending on the sale price and number of cows safely delivered to market. When assigned to a line shack for the winter, to keep an eye on distant herds, a cowboy might take a string of "rough" horses with him and receive a bonus for breaking them. That brings us to another myth. Horses were not broken in bucking contests out in the old corral. They were bucked out in soft sand or knee-deep water to give the rider an advantage.

Few Americans know the major role Europeans played in the development of the U.S. cattle industry. Foreign ownership of large cattle spreads was common. By 1883, the English alone had invested more than $45 million in the U.S. cattle business and owned 20 million acres of grazing land. One Texas ranch, owned by a Scotsman, covered 500,000 acres. The Dutch and Germans also invested heavily in the cattle business. There were two reasons for foreign interest in the American West.

PART
FIVE
*The Vikings,
Belle Starr,
and Lucky
Lindy*

Outlaw or petty thief?
Belle Starr was
recreated in magazine
accounts and dime
novels as an outlaw
queen.
Mercaldo Archives

The first was the great depression of 1873, which drastically changed the character of the industry. The depression devastated the railroad companies, forced banks to close, and put a large number of cattlemen out of business. After that, U.S. bankers were reluctant to invest money in anything so speculative as the cattle business. The second motivating factor was a book written by James S. Brisbin, titled *The Beef Bonanza; or How to Get Rich on the Plains.* It became the investment "Bible" for enterprising Europeans, who formed large co-ops, purchased vast tracts and huge herds, and sent accountants to America to manage their cattle empires.

In contrast to these foreign-owned enterprises, most American-owned ranches were modest spreads worked by a family and two or three hired hands.

The American West was a strangely paradoxical place. Although there was racial intolerance, the West also was a place where a man often was judged by what he did rather than the hue of his skin. On a working ranch, an Indian who could rope was accorded the respect due his skills. A Mexican who could break mean horses with soothing words was highly regarded. And, for a time, a Black man named Bill Pickett was considered the greatest cowboy alive. A top hand at the famous 101 Ranch in Oklahoma, he is credited with inventing bulldogging. Instead of roping steers for

★

That's
Not
in My
American
History
Book

200

branding, Bill simply grabbed them by the horns and threw them to the ground. Early in the twentieth century, he went on the Wild West show circuit to demonstrate the technique. Today bulldogging (or steer wrestling) is a competitive event in rodeos.

Race did not prevent Nat Love, the son of Tennessee slaves, from becoming a legendary figure in the west. Love is better known in western lore as Deadwood Dick. In his teens, he ran away from home and worked for several Texas ranchers, becoming highly skilled with rope and six-gun.

By his own description, he was "wild, reckless, free and afraid of nothing." Describing his life in later years, he admitted wasting a lot of his youth, "dancin', drinkin' and shootin' up the town." But in spite of his wild and independent nature, if Nat Love gave his word to deliver a herd of cattle, a rancher could be certain the herd would arrive.

In 1876, Love delivered 3,000 head of cows to miners in South Dakota, then went into the town of Deadwood to celebrate. Arriving on the Fourth of July, Love found a celebration already in progress. Local gamblers had raised prize money for roping and shooting contests. Love entered, easily won both competitions and from that day he was called Deadwood Dick. Embellished stories about him spread throughout the West, and the legend of Deadwood Dick soon outpaced even the deeds of the man.

An eastern writer named Edward L. Wheeler heard the stories and penned a novel rather grandly titled *Deadwood Dick, the Prince of the Road, or the Black Rider of the Black Hills*. It was the first of thirty-three Deadwood Dick novels. In Wheeler's books, Deadwood Dick was a dashing hero who wore black clothes, black boots, black hat, and rode a black horse. There was only one thing white about Wheeler's Deadwood Dick—his skin. Out West, the real Nat Love was a legend in his own right; but back East, in order to be a legend, he had to be White.

The Civil War that gave birth to the cattle industry and the American cowboy also spawned the outlaw gangs of the wild wild west. For a generation of young men, the war was their only education. This was especially so in those states west of the Mississippi River where guerrilla warfare prevailed. Loose-knit Confederate military units, known as partisan rangers early in the war, evolved into nothing more than outlaw bands in its latter stages. The James brothers of Missouri spent their teen years raiding and killing with William Quantrill's guerrilla band. At the end of the war, their

Some cowboys were Indians
Osage and Pawnee Indians were valued for their herding skills. Few were as grandly attired as this Osage cowboy.
University of Oklahoma Press, Norman, Oklahoma

entry into outlawry was a natural progression. In fact, their early robberies were carried out like military operations.

Although the Jesse James gang was the most notorious of the post–Civil War outlaws, the pattern of armed criminal activity was repeated throughout the South and Southwest. In Louisiana, the Red West gang terrorized the state until two soldiers were killed in a payroll robbery, inspiring authorities to hunt down the leaders and hang them. In Texas, Sam Bass led a gang of ex-Confederates who robbed stages, trains, and banks until Texas Rangers ambushed and killed him at Round Rock.

By the 1880s most of the outlaw gangs had been wiped out. It was never so glamorous an occupation as Hollywood would have us believe. The working conditions included sleeping on the ground in all kinds of weather and being shot at by large groups of heavily armed and angry men. And the pay was not that great. In all of his robberies, Jesse James managed to steal only about $90,000.

Many other western myths cry for correction. The most obvious one is the image of a cowboy strutting around with a six-shooter on his hip. Working cowboys rarely wore pistols. Those

⭐

**That's
Not
in My
American
History
Book**

who happened to own pistols kept them stashed in saddlebags or bedrolls. Cowboys were working men, and a gun on their hip only got in the way. Occasionally, a cowpoke might strap on his pistol and ride into town, wearing it for protection or to shoot a rattlesnake in his path. But any cowboy caught swaggering around the old bunkhouse with a gun buckled on his waist probably would have been told to pack his gear and hit the road.

So what about those high noon, quick-draw, main street shootouts? They simply did not happen until Hollywood invented them. In Hollywood, every cowboy is a gunfighter. In the real West, gunfights were rare. When they did occur, the combatants were more likely to hide behind trees and buildings to shoot at each other than to stand in the open. In his autobiography, famed lawman Wyatt Earp noted that he would never attempt to outdraw an adversary, pointing out that one stood a much better chance of survival if he simply took careful aim and fired. In the Wild West, an ability to "get the drop" on an adversary was much more important than a quick draw.

Western lore records Tom Horn as a legendary, quick-shooting gunfighter. In real life, he was a hired killer who usually shot his victims from ambush. He always placed a small rock beneath the head of his victim as a trademark to prove the job was his and assure payment by his employer. He was successful in this enterprise until someone else placed a rock beneath the head of a murder victim and Horn was blamed for the crime. He proclaimed his innocence even as he went through a gallows trapdoor with a rope around his neck. Later it was discovered that Horn might not have been guilty of the crime after all, but there was a general feeling by then that he probably had it coming anyway.

There were some downright mean characters out West, just as there are today. One of them was a Texan named John Wesley Hardin, who was credited with killing more than forty men, although most historians place the number at eight. One of those victims was a man Hardin supposedly shot because he would not stop snoring.

So just how wild was the Wild West?

Back in the 1970s, Craig Miner, a professor at Wichita State University, conducted a study of violent behavior in the West of the nineteenth century, compared it to crime statistics in the twentieth century, and concluded that per capita homicide rates in today's western states far exceed those of the fabled Wild West era.

The reason, he stated, was because citizens back then would not tolerate the kind of street violence taken for granted today.

At the height of the California gold rush, San Francisco averaged two murders a day until vigilante groups cleaned up the city. When a visiting cowboy gunned down an unarmed citizen in Wichita, Kansas, local officials were so outraged they brought in Wyatt Earp to clean up the town. Earp might have been amused by today's debate on gun control. He carried his own gun control law on his hip. Anyone entering a town where Earp enforced the law had to turn in his weapon before entering the city limits. When it became necessary for him to face down a drunken cowboy, Earp was more inclined to use his wit than his six-shooter to effect an arrest.

According to Miner, Earp spent most of his time in Wichita inspecting chimneys for fire hazards, sweeping the sidewalks, and picking up dead animals. If Earp had to patrol Wichita's streets today, he might turn in his badge. Like many modern cities, Wichita has its share of street violence resulting in the kind of drive-by ambushes usually associated with the old West.

The wild, wild west? It's now.

The original gangstas Jesse and Frank James (first and second from left) led one of the most feared outlaw gangs in the West.

Each spring, a new generation of bright young graduates depart our secondary schools, boldly looking to the future, proudly clutching their diplomas, and firmly believing that Charles Lindbergh was the first person to fly across the Atlantic Ocean.

Charles Augustus Lindbergh was not the first to fly an aircraft across the Atlantic. He also was not the second. He might have been the 82nd. One cannot be certain, because of conflicting reports on the number of crew members aboard some of the several flights that preceded him.

The first transatlantic flight in a fixed-wing aircraft took place in 1919 when Lindbergh was only seventeen years old. It was accomplished by Lt. Commander Albert (Putty) Read and a crew of five. They made the crossing in a U.S. Navy Curtiss "flying boat" christened the *Lame Duck*.

Read and his crew left Rockaway Air Station at Long Island, New York, on May 16, 1919 and flew to Trepassey Bay, Newfoundland. From there they took off for Europe. Unfortunately, once in the air, the *Lame Duck* performed to the level of its name. Two of the aircraft's four engines failed, forcing the *Lame Duck* to spend more time sitting in the water than it did flying in the air. The crew suffered alternating bouts of air and sea sickness, because much time was spent with the aircraft rocking in the ocean waves while the mechanics worked on its engines.

The *Lame Duck* finally made it to Lisbon, Portugal, following a stop in the Azores. From Lisbon, Read flew to Plymouth, England, arriving there on May 27. The entire journey covered 3,936 miles. Read returned to the United States a national hero; but even before he arrived back home, his record had been eclipsed by two British aviators.

Just three weeks after Read landed his reluctant craft at Plymouth, Cpt. John Alcock and his copilot, Lt. Arthur Brown, took off from St. Johns, Newfoundland, in a converted World War I bomber, headed for England. Their goal was to accomplish the first nonstop flight across the Atlantic; and they had no choice but to complete it, because the Vickers Night Bomber they piloted was not amphibious. The only alternative to success was a watery grave at the bottom of the ocean. The flight turned into an incredible adventure filled with danger and suspense.

Shortly after taking off on June 14, 1919, they flew into a thick fog. Disoriented, Alcock almost dived the plane into the ocean. They were only a few feet above the water when he discovered their predicament and barely avoided disaster. Next they encountered a blinding snowstorm, and ice began collecting on the plane, making it difficult to control. Left with little choice, Brown climbed onto the wings to chip away the ice even as Alcock fought the controls to keep the vibrating craft aloft. Miraculously, they managed to stay airborne through the night and landed the following day at Clifden, England.

A British military dirigible was the next craft to cross the Atlantic. Maj. G. Scott commanded the four-day flight from East Fortune, Scotland, to Mineola, New York, in July of 1919. Aboard was a crew of thirty crewmen, plus some British government officials and one stowaway—a crewman who had been bumped from the flight but refused to be left behind. Upon arriving at Mineola, the dirigible encountered high winds that made landing dangerous. A crew member had to parachute to the ground to direct the landing.

In 1924, three years before Lindbergh's flight, two members of the U.S. Army Air Service, flying separate aircraft, managed to complete an incredible around-the-world flight. They were Lt. Lowell H. Smith and Lt. Erik H. Nelson. Flying amphibious Douglas military airplanes, they took off from Seattle, Washington, on April 24 and hopscotched from islands to continents. They made fifty-seven stops on a trip that covered 26,100 miles, finally returning to Seattle on September 28.

In October of 1924, a large German airship crossed the Atlantic with thirty-four men on board and docked at Lakehurst, New Jersey. The flight was scheduled as a goodwill mission to improve relations between Germany and the United States. To that end, the Germans christened their craft the *Los Angeles*.

More than a year before Lindbergh made his famous 1927

That's
Not
in My
American
History
Book

flight, a Spaniard named Ramon Franco and two crew members flew a twin-engine flying boat from Palos, Spain, to Buenos Aires, Argentina, becoming the first to fly across the South Atlantic. Franco was hailed as the "Columbus of the Air" in South America, but his feat received only passing mention in North American newspapers.

In February of 1927, an Italian named Francesco Marquis de Pinedo and two assistants flew a seaplane named the *Santa Maria* from Italy to Pernambuco, Brazil. De Pinedo then flew the craft to the United States for a planned goodwill mission tour. Unfortunately, the tour was cut short by an incident that created a diplomatic nightmare for the U.S. State Department.

When de Pinedo landed the *Santa Maria* on a lake in Arizona to take on fuel, the aircraft attracted a large crowd. In the crowd was a teenage onlooker who happened to light a cigarette and casually flipped the match into the water. The match ignited fuel that had spilled beneath the airplane, and the *Santa Maria* went up in a ball of flame as the anguished de Pinedo and his crewman watched helplessly.

Outraged Italian officials promptly accused the United States of sabotaging the *Santa Maria* as part of an anti-Fascist plot against the Italian government. The diplomatic squabble continued for weeks before an investigation finally convinced the Italians the fire was started by accident.

On June 27, 1927, Charles Lindbergh finally took off in his *Spirit of St. Louis* monoplane from Roosevelt Field at Long Island, New York. Thirty-three hours later he landed at La Bourget, just outside Paris, France. He was puzzled to be greeted by a massive, wildly cheering crowd. Unknown to Lindbergh, almost everyone in France had been clustered around radios for hours, collectively holding their breaths as announcers dramatically reported the progress of his flight. In an outpouring of relief and emotion, thousands rushed to the landing site. They lifted Lindbergh from his airplane, and he later noted that it was thirty minutes before his feet touched the ground. Souvenir hunters descended on the aircraft, ripping away fabric, taking instruments, and even making off with engine parts.

The drama that surrounded the Lindbergh flight made him a hero of legendary status in Europe as well as the United States. But he was not the first to fly across the Atlantic. Nor was he the first to fly nonstop across the ocean. He was the first to fly alone across the ocean.

A head count of pilots, crews, and passengers aboard the various aircraft that preceded him indicate that at least eighty-one individuals flew across the Atlantic before Lindbergh. There might have been more. But none would reap the glory heaped upon the shy young American aviator thay called "Lucky Lindy."

Little known is the fact that Lindbergh almost did not make the flight at all. William P. MacCracken, a U.S. government aeronautics official, came close to grounding Lindbergh as a dangerous pilot shortly before the flight. MacCracken based his charges on Lindbergh's involvement in numerous aviation accidents. As a mail pilot and barnstormer, Lindbergh had bailed out of airplanes on four occasions and survived several other mishaps. Lindbergh's sponsors finally talked MacCracken into delaying any action until after the flight. By then there was no way MacCracken could ground a legend.

The Truth behind the Boston Tea Party

When the British raised the price of tea, Boston citizens were so outraged they disguised themselves as Indians, went down to the docks, boarded British ships, and dumped their cargoes of tea into the harbor. We all know that story. We learned it in school. But that is not exactly how it happened.

The Boston Tea Party did not take place because the British raised the price of tea, but because the British East India Company lowered the price. It was not a spontaneous event as depicted in our history texts, but a carefully planned demonstration organized by "patriots" who stood to lose a great deal of money if cheap British tea was dumped on the American market. And finally, thanks to a rum party that preceded the tea party, many of the participants were so drunk they passed out before completing their task.

Boston was not the only place to hold a tea party. There also were tea protests at New York Harbor; Greenwich, Connecticut; Philadelphia, Pennsylvania; Charleston, South Carolina; and a most spectacular one at Annapolis, Maryland. There, demonstrators kidnapped a ship's captain, set his vessel on fire, and made him watch as it went up in flames.

Why all of the excitement over tea?

The great tea conflict began when the British East India Company hiked its prices to accommodate tax increases levied by the crown. The result was the evolution of a thriving black market in tea in the colonies. Enterprising Americans began importing contraband tea from the Netherlands and selling it well below the price of British tea. Supposedly, some of our most revered patriots were involved in this illicit but profitable trade.

As more and more Americans refused to drink British tea, the East India Company faced a financial crisis. It became so overstocked with unsold tea, there was a seven-year supply sitting in warehouses in England.

PART
FIVE
*The Vikings,
Belle Starr,
and Lucky
Lindy*

209

Who's giving the party? The Boston Tea Party and similar demonstrations were neither spontaneous acts nor purely patriotic protests. *National Archives & Records Administration*

To unload some of that stock and eliminate competition in the colonies, it was decided the company would slash its prices below black market costs. But when shiploads of cheap British tea arrived in the colonies, Americans reacted in an unexpected way. Instead of being pleased, they were angry. Colonial tea-drinkers felt they were being manipulated by the British; but little did they realize, they also were being manipulated by the black marketers, who organized a series of "spontaneous" tea parties.

Although the British managed to unload tea at some ports, three ships laden with tea remained at anchor in Boston Harbor, threatened with sabotage if crews tried to bring their cargoes ashore.

A group of colonial leaders, led by Samuel Adams, urged Governor Thomas Hutchinson of Massachusetts to avoid conflict by prohibiting the English from unloading the tea. Hutchinson refused, and on December 16, 1773, the day before the tea was to come ashore, Adams staged an anti-tea rally. A crowd of 8,000 showed up, which was remarkable considering that was about half the population of Boston. Even as he spoke to the crowd, Adams received word that the governor had a refused a final request to stop the unloading. At that point, Adams turned to the crowd and dramatically announced:

"There is nothing more this meeting can do to save the country."

That's
Not
in My
American
History
Book

It was around 4 o'clock that same afternoon when another crowd gathered at the home of Boston businessman Benjamin Edes. The meeting was organized by the local Committee of Correspondence, and present were some fifty carefully chosen men in addition to several leaders of the organization. They were there to lead an assault on the British ships.

To fortify their resolve, Edes placed a massive punch bowl on a table and filled it with a potent rum concoction. His son, Peter, was given the job of keeping the bowl filled. Years later, Peter Edes would write that the consumption rate that day was such that he was hard-pressed to fulfill his duty.

By 6 P.M., Samuel Adams had rallied a huge crowd at the docks at Griffin's Wharf. Also at the docks, not knowing what to expect, were nervous British officials and representatives of the East India Company.

As darkness descended on the waterfront, the men from the Edes party arrived, some dressed as Indians, some visibly staggering, and all in a festive mood. Joining them at the docks were members of other patriotic organizations. To the cheers of the crowd and the horror of the helpless British onlookers, the raiders boarded the tea ships.

It required three hours for the intruders to dump the cargoes overboard. The task might have been completed sooner, but a substantial number of the dumpers became violently ill and had to retire from the proceedings.

Back in England, government officials were outraged and reacted by passing an act to close Boston Harbor. They vowed to keep it closed and limit self-rule in Massachusetts until the colonists paid for the tea they had destroyed. To enforce the act, additional troops were assigned to Boston.

Rather than suppress the Colonial rebellion, the British reaction served only to intensify it and shove the Colonials and their mother country toward an inevitable armed conflict.

The First Flag Maker?

Betsy Ross was a truly remarkable woman. She was a loving mother and dutiful wife who outlived three husbands. In an era when women were suppressed, she was an astute businesswoman who acquired land holdings and livestock worth a small fortune. And, of course, she was a whiz with a needle and thread. But she did not make the first American flag.

She was born Elizabeth Grisom, one of seventeen children raised in a Quaker family in Philadelphia. Her mother taught her needlework, at which she became adept while still a young girl.

She married John Ross in 1773 and, three years later, was widowed when he was killed in an explosion on the Philadelphia waterfront. A year later, she married Joseph Ashburn, the first mate of the brigantine *Patty*. They had two children; but in 1781 her second husband's ship was captured by the British, and he died in prison in London.

When her first husband died, Betsy had established an upholstery and sewing shop. Because her second husband was away at sea for extended periods, she supported herself and her children with profits from the shop. As part of her sewing business, she did make flags, but they were for ships' colors and local militia units.

She wisely managed her finances and eventually acquired 190 acres of land in Cumberland and Philadelphia counties. She stocked her land with carefully selected, fine-blooded livestock. In 1782, she married John Claypool, and they lived together until his death in 1817. She eventually raised seven children and, at age eighty-four, died in obscurity. That, in capsule form, is the life of Betsy Ross. Her name would have remained obscured by time if not for a grandson named William Canby.

In March of 1870, almost a century after the American Revolution and fourteen years after the death of Betsy Ross, Canby gave a speech before the Philadelphia Historical Society. He stated

★

That's
Not
in My
American
History
Book

212

that his grandmother had been visited by George Washington and commissioned to make the first American flag bearing the stars and stripes. Although Canby offered no evidence to back his claim, the story was published in *Harper's Magazine*. Incredibly, by the mid 1880s, the story had gained such wide acceptance it was being printed as fact in school books.

Based on Canby's story, Charles H. Weisberger, a noted artist of the period, completed a painting titled *Birth of Our Nation's Flag*. It depicted Betsy Ross displaying a finished stars-and-stripes flag to an approving George Washington. The painting was unveiled at the World Columbian Exposition at Chicago in 1893 and viewed by hundreds of thousands of visitors. Weisberger's work firmly established the myth and his painting appeared in school textbooks for years, deceiving generations of unsuspecting students.

There was never any evidence to support Canby's story, but a great deal to refute it. Canby claimed his grandmother was visited by Washington in 1776, and she made the flag in time for it to be unfurled before the Continental Congress meeting at Independence Hall in Philadelphia. However, the flag bearing the stars and stripes was not even designed until 1777. It was first drawn by an artist named Francis Hopkinson from a design probably suggested by Washington, since the flag was similar to the Washington fam-

Sewing the Stars and Stripes Though it makes a colorful story, there is no proof that Betsy Ross sewed the nation's first flag. *National Archives & Records Administration*

ily's English coat of arms, which included three stars set above red and white stripes.

The very first stars-and-stripes flag probably was hastily sewn by the defenders of Fort Schuyler at Rome, New York, in August of 1777. Such a flag, believed to have been made from garments donated by the soldiers, was flown over the fort at the time. It contained thirteen stars and thirteen red and white stripes representing the colonies.

It would be almost a half-century later before the flag was christened "Old Glory." That was the name given it by William Diver, a sea captain from Salem, Massachusetts. In 1824, he hoisted a homemade flag sewn by his mother on his ship the *Charles Doggett*, saluted, and said: "I name thee Old Glory."

The only documented evidence that Betsy Ross ever made a flag of any kind is found in the minutes of the Pennsylvania State Navy Board. It shows a payment to Elizabeth Ross for making "ship's colors."

Why Canby persisted with his story, and why it was not challenged at the time of its inception, remains a mystery. But there is little doubt the legend will continue. So ingrained in our history is the name Betsy Ross that high school students taking tests sometimes identify her as the wife of George Washington.

The Much-Maligned Lynch

> lynch (linch) v. (lynch law): to put to death by mob action
> without legal sanction.
>
> *Webster's New Collegiate Dictionary*

Few men have been more ill treated by history than Charles Lynch. His very name has come to define execution without benefit of justice, and that in itself is an injustice to the man. It is ironic that a man who once judged others with reason and compassion should later be so harshly judged by history.

Lynch was a rural justice of the peace in Virginia during the American Revolution. As the war spread south into Virginia, he was dismayed to witness the breakdown in law and order that accompanied it. And one of the most lawless regions of the state was his own Bedford County.

The conflict between British Loyalists and Colonials had created an atmosphere in which the courts simply ceased to function. Guerrilla bands and militias on both sides roamed the countryside, and hooligans often ruled the streets. Finally, Lynch decided to take the law into his own hands. He did so by setting up his own unofficial court, appointing law officers, and ordering the arrest of lawbreakers. Because there were no funds available for the jailing and care of prisoners, Lynch was limited to the kinds of punishment he could impose on those found guilty in his self-styled court. He assessed fines for minor infractions and ordered whippings for those found guilty of more serious crimes. This rather crude form of punishment proved effective. No one wanted to end up in Judge Lynch's court. But it also created a great deal of animosity against Lynch among the families of the recipients of his punishments.

With the end of the war, the legend of Charles Lynch spread far beyond the borders of Virginia, and the stories became more outlandish with each retelling. According to the myth, he was an indiscriminate hangman.

Actually, Lynch imposed the death penalty only once. It was in an espionage case that would haunt him to his grave and darken his name forever.

The case began when Col. William Campbell of the Continental Army uncovered a plot by Tories to destroy the lead mines near Fort Criswell, Virginia. The lead mines were vital to the Revolutionary War effort. The plotters were arrested and brought before Lynch, who admittedly faced a dilemma if not a conflict of interest. Not only was he the judge in the case, he also had an interest in the lead mines. The conspirators were found guilty and Lynch ordered them hanged.

Following the war, friends and relatives of the condemned men, along with others who had faced Lynch in his court complained to authorities about his unorthodox judgments and sentences. The complaints resulted in a government investigation of Lynch's activities.

In 1782, the investigative panel made its report. It was concluded that Lynch was justified in sentencing the conspirators to death because they presented a clear danger to the State of Virginia in a time of war. The panel also cleared Lynch of wrongdoing in the other cases and, in fact, commended him for bringing law and order to Bedford County.

Although exonerated, Charles Lynch had become a controversial figure. His name eventually would symbolize vigilante justice or, more precisely, illegal execution.

The practice of vigilante groups dispensing "lynch law" became common in California during the lawlessness that accompanied the gold rush in the early 1850s. Scores of suspects were hanged without benefit of trial, and some, no doubt, were innocent.

In the last half of the nineteenth century, American justice went haywire. By the 1880s, illegal hangings were common in the western states, where the nearest law might be days away and accusers were not inclined to wait for the appearance of a territorial marshal or circuit judge. In some locales, to be caught stealing a horse or cow or cutting a fence was an automatic death sentence.

However, most of the "lynchings" of the period took place in the South, where African-Americans were the victims. With the end of Reconstruction and the departure of federal troops from the South, radical whites began seeking revenge for real or imagined offenses committed by blacks. The result was a rash of racially motivated lynchings.

That's
Not
in My
American
History
Book

From 1882 until the present, there have been almost 5,000 lynchings in the United States, most of them taking place in a 40-year period between 1885 and 1925. In each case, these horrible perversions of justice were carried out under the name of the man who once struggled to bring law and order to Bedford County, Virginia.

Nathan Hale's Famous Last Words

Just before he was to be hanged by the British for being a spy, Nathan Hale was asked if he had any final words. Supposedly, he replied: "I only regret that I have but one life to give for my country."

Those stirring words of dedication to duty and love of country have been a source of inspiration to succeeding generations of Hale's countrymen. Regrettably, he probably never said them. In fact, those famous last words, long attributed to Nathan Hale, probably came from the pen of a newspaper reporter rather than the lips of the patriot himself.

This much we know about the events surrounding Hale's execution:

On the night of September 21, 1776, he was captured by British soldiers in New York after being betrayed by a relative. Under questioning, Hale confessed to being a spy for the Continental Army. In fact, there was little reason for him to lie to his captors since incriminating papers were found on his person. Upon hearing the evidence against Hale, British general Sir William Howe ordered his execution by hanging the following morning.

The only official record of the event appears in Howe's logs for the date of September 22, 1776.

> A spy from the enemy by his own full confession, apprehended late last night, was executed this date at 11 o'clock in front of the Artillery Park.

An unofficial version was provided by a British Army lieutenant named Frederick McKenzie. He wrote the following account of the event in his journal:

> He [Hale] behaved with great resolution, saying he

★

That's
Not
in My
American
History
Book

thought it the duty of every good officer to obey any orders given him by his commander in chief . . . He desired the spectators to be at all times prepared to meet death in whatever shape it might appear.

Nathan Hale was only twenty-one years old when he died. He had only recently graduated from Yale University. Dedicated to the Colonial cause, he offered his services to General George Washington.

Following the defeat of Washington's forces on Long Island, Hale volunteered to remain behind enemy lines and gather information on British troop movements for the Colonial Army. Papers detailing the deployment of British forces were found when he was taken into custody and later used as evidence against him.

Hale made only two requests of his captors before being hanged. He asked to have a clergyman of his choice at his execution, and he requested that a letter he had written to his mother be delivered. However, General Howe was not in a compassionate mood. He refused Hale's request for a clergyman and ordered the letter destroyed. In doing so, Howe helped solidify opposition to the British Army and fueled the legend that would grow from the death of the young spy from Yale.

The famous quotation attributed to Nathan Hale appeared in print for the first time five months after his death when published in a Massachusetts newspaper. It became an inspiration to his fellow revolutionaries. However, in all likelihood, those precise words were never uttered from the gallows at Artillery Park that morning. They were penned by a patriotic newspaper reporter long after Hale was in his grave.

The Discovery of America, and Other Columbus Myths

There are so many myths surrounding Christopher Columbus and his explorations that one hardly knows where to begin refuting them. The most significant fact is that he did not discover America. In fact, there are maps, journals, documents, and written histories to indicate that numerous expeditions reached the Americas before Columbus, not to mention the many migrations of nomadic hunters from Asia.

There is no doubt that Norse seamen were exploring the shores of North America hundreds of years before Columbus was born. Between 986 and 1356 A.D., at least five Norse expeditions are believed to have reached the "New World." There are even indications that a Norse colony of woodcutters shipped timber from present-day Nova Scotia to Greenland more than a hundred years before Columbus came on the scene. But the Norse were not alone in their curiosity about a great land mass across the ocean, beyond the setting sun.

Maritime and merchants' records at Bristol, England, indicate that ships were being outfitted for journeys to lands to the west in the 1480s. Some of these vessels are believed to have been fishing the coastal waters of North America a decade before Columbus set sail.

Seldom acknowledged is the claim by a Danish navigator named Deitrich Pining that he reached North America in 1472. Inspired by Pining's accounts of a land to the west, King Alfonso of Portugal and King Christian I of Denmark sponsored a joint expedition to North America in 1477. Their objective was not to colonize the new land, but to find a passage through it to the riches of the Far East. Chosen to lead the expedition were a Danish sea captain named Johannes Scolp and a Portuguese nobleman known only as Joao Corte Real (Joao of the Royal Court). It is believed

That's
Not
in My
American
History
Book

220

Scolp and Joao crossed the North Atlantic and explored the coast of Labrador, Hudson Bay, and the St. Lawrence River before returning home. Because they did not find a water route to Asia, the voyage was considered a failure and little noted by historians. However, it might help explain why King John II of Portugal later refused to finance a proposed voyage by Columbus. The Portuguese had already been there and done that.

So how did Pining, Scolp and Joao know they would encounter a land mass to the west? They knew because the Norse had been telling stories about its existence for 500 years. But even the Vikings might have been late visitors to the continent.

There are ancient Chinese writings chronicling at least two visits to the western shores of North America, beginning at a time when the Egyptians were just starting to build a canal system and the Minoans were developing a civilization on Crete.

The first Chinese visit to the Americas supposedly took place about 2540 B.C. when two imperial astronomers were sent forth with instructions to explore distant lands. It is believed they sailed north, hopscotching the coast of Asia; they then crossed the Bering Strait and sailed southward along the coast of North America. Subsequent events indicate they could have traveled all the way to Central America before returning via the same route.

In 458 A.D., a Chinese Buddhist priest named Hui Shun is believed to have used ancient imperial documents that descended from the two astronomers to retrace their route to the west coast of Central America. Hui Shun remained in the Americas (possibly in what is now Mexico) for more than forty years before returning to China in 502 A.D. to record his adventures and report his findings to the Emperor Wu.

On the other side of the world, two medieval manuscripts in Iceland detail a journey by Saint Brendan of Ireland who, with seventeen other monks, embarked on a seven-year voyage that supposedly took them down the Atlantic coastline of North America, all the way to Grand Cayman Island. According to legend, this journey, begun in 550 A.D., was undertaken in a leather-hulled boat called a "curragh."

Saint Brendan named the continent to the west, "The Land Promised to the Saints." He returned to Iceland in 557 and chronicled his travels. Unfortunately, Saint Brendan had a streak of fiction in his soul, leading scholars to conclude his journey was short on fact. In 1977, however, an Irishman named Timothy Severin

PART
FIVE
The Vikings,
Belle Starr,
and Lucky
Lindy

221

Marketer of America
Christopher Columbus
may not have
discovered America,
but he sold Europe on
it as a source of riches
and power.
Eric Schaal

used a curragh to sail across the North Atlantic and retrace the route described by Saint Brendan, proving to skeptics that such a voyage was possible. One fact is inescapable: Saint Brendan and his party, having disappeared for seven years, must have traveled somewhere.

There are other written claims of pre-Columbian trips to the Americas. A Welsh prince reportedly died in North America while attempting to start a colony. That was in 1190, some 300 years before Columbus. And, according to Arab historical and geographical documents, a black Muslim king named Abubakari II, upon hearing of a land across the sea, had a large boat constructed of reeds. He sailed from the coast of Africa in 1311 and simply followed prevailing currents. It is believed he and his crew made landfall on the north coast of South America and eventually made their way to near present-day Panama. From there they journeyed overland and eventually settled in a great nation—possibly the Mayan Empire. The well-publicized, transatlantic Ra expeditions of the twentieth century, undertaken by European sailors who followed the ocean currents in reed boats built by West Africans, proved that Abubakari II's voyage was possible.

Did the great Phoenician sailors reach North America? Although there is no evidence to support such a supposition, they certainly possessed the skill and daring to have done so. They had

**That's
Not
in My
American
History
Book**

222

sailed to the British Isles and rounded the tip of Africa 2,000 years before Columbus was born.

Adding to the mystery is the recent discovery in North America of human remains, dating to 12,000 years ago, that do not seem to be of Asiatic origin. The structure of the skulls is more indicative of European origin than Asian. The theory that Europeans might have found their way to the Americas at such an early date is being vigorously challenged by Native Americans. The cultures and religions of some tribes are based on the supposition that they are the only true natives of the continent. Their insistence that archaeologists and anthropologists not disturb the burial sites of their ancestors has led to recent court battles between scientists and Native Americans.

So if Columbus did not discover America, why all the fuss over him? He is important because he opened the door to the Americas and blocked it with his foot. Part visionary and part snake-oil salesman, he whetted the greed of the Spanish monarchy, the church, unscrupulous noblemen, and bureaucratic speculators with promises of great wealth from distant lands. As mythical as the riches he described were the myths that would surround the man. Here are the facts about some of the most common Columbus myths:

☞ He was hardly alone in his belief that the Earth was round. It had been accepted fact among men of learning for more than 200 years before he was born. The fable that Columbus wanted to prove the Earth was round came from the imagination of Washington Irving, whose biography on the explorer appeared in 1828.

☞ Columbus did not embark on his journey out of a sense of adventure or for the sake of discovery. He went seeking those things that have motivated men throughout history—wealth, fame, and power.

☞ Columbus did not think he had reached India when he landed on Watling Island. He thought he had reached Malaysia. His initial explorations were aimed at finding a passage to the Indian Ocean through what he believed were the islands of the Malaysian Peninsula. Only later did he consider that he might have discovered a new land mass between Europe and Asia.

☞ Columbus's ancestry and early life are cloaked in a mystery of his own creation. Although he claimed to have been born in Italy, he might have been of Spanish descent. He used the surname Colon instead of the Italian Colombo or the Latin Columbus. He could not read or write Latin. He lived most of his life in Spain and Portugal and, as a young sailor, fought against the Italians. Some historians believe he might have been Jewish. At the time Columbus was reaching adulthood, Spain was persecuting its Jews and pressuring them to convert to Christianity, and it is possible Columbus wanted to conceal his background.

⭐

PART
FIVE
The Vikings,
Belle Starr,
and Lucky
Lindy

223

☛ The real reason Columbus had difficulty acquiring financial backing for his first voyage was not a scarcity of funds so much as his own arrogance. Before undertaking his voyage, he insisted on being named Admiral of the Ocean Sea. He wanted to become viceroy of all lands he might claim for Spain on his journey and insisted that he be paid ten percent of all income derived from the enterprise.

☛ Queen Isabella of Spain did not pawn her jewels to pay for Columbus's first voyage. In fact, no royal family funds were used. Financing for the venture was arranged by the treasurer of the royal household, who used some of his own personal funds. However, the bulk of the monies came from a loan secured from a fund belonging to the royal police force.

☛ Contrary to popular belief, Columbus was not a favorite of the Queen. In fact, she did not like him very much, and King Ferdinand could hardly stand him at all. They tolerated Columbus because he represented their best hope for beating Portugal to the riches of Asia. Although they agreed to some of his demands for titles and compensation, they had no intention of honoring them.

☛ Columbus and his little three-vessel fleet did not encounter great storms on that storied first voyage. In fact, the seas were calm and the crossing uneventful until the final day before landfall, when they experienced some rough waters. After leaving Palos, Spain, the fleet spent a month anchored in the Canary Islands before making the crossing, which required less than a month, not the two months claimed in most history texts.

☛ There was no threatened mutiny by the crew. At one point, Columbus and the Pinzon brothers (who captained the two sister ships) did meet to discuss whether they should continue or turn back. They decided to continue and reassess the situation in a few days.

☛ Columbus did not alter his logs to mislead others into thinking

★

That's
Not
in My
American
History
Book

224

they had sailed a shorter distance than was actually the case. His navigators and helmsmen were experienced seamen who would have detected such a ruse. Also, it would have been necessary for him to fool the Pinzon brothers, who were far superior to Columbus as navigators.

☞ Long ignored by history is that Columbus was a brutal conqueror and slave trader. In 1493, upon his return to Hispaniola (the island that would become Haiti and the Dominican Republic) he subdued the Arawak natives, slaughtering thousands in the process. With an army of 200 well-armed Spaniards, he forced the Arawaks to search for gold, provide spun cotton for shipment to Spain, and grow food for his troops. He demanded that each native turn in a quota of gold each month. Those who did not meet their quotas were subject to having their hands chopped off to inspire others to work harder. Frustrated by the Arawaks' inability to produce large quantities of gold, Columbus established a slave trade, sending hundreds of native Americans to Spain. Few survived the ocean voyage. Those who did not die at sea quickly became victims of European diseases.

☞ When Columbus rebelled against royal family representatives on Hispaniola, he was arrested, placed in irons, and sent back to Spain in disgrace. Pardoned by the King and Queen, he was sent forth on new voyages to find new lands to exploit. Unfortunately, Columbus's brutal subjugation of the natives on Hispaniola established a pattern for Spanish exploitation with slave labor in the New World for the next 200 years.

☞ Finally, it might be noted that Columbus did not die penniless and unappreciated, as history would have us believe. Thanks to the then-recent development of the printing press, he became a famous personality in his lifetime. Although not exceedingly wealthy, he was financially comfortable at the time of his death. His son inherited his funds and titles.

Columbus made four voyages, opening the door to a world that would make Spain the most powerful nation on Earth for a time. He spent his final years bent by arthritis and bitter at the royal family for real or imagined wrongs. He died in 1506, just fourteen years after his first voyage. A year after his death, a mapmaker, needing a name for the new land to the west, named it America (for Amerigo Vespucci), which no doubt would have been a blow to Columbus's enormous ego.

It should be noted that when Columbus set foot on Hispaniola to claim it for Spain, it is believed as many as ten million natives might have inhabited the island. At the time of his death, fewer than 20,000 enslaved natives remained there. In 1517, large deposits of gold were discovered on Hispaniola. Native slaves from surrounding islands and Florida had to be brought in to work the mines. By the 1550s there were no natives left on the island, and enslaved Africans were being imported to replace them in the fields and mines.

There is one final, ironic footnote to the Columbus story. That first historic voyage was not even necessary for its intended purpose of finding an ocean route to India. Even before Columbus sailed, a Portuguese sailor named Bartolomeu Dias had rounded the tip of Africa. In 1498, Vasco da Gama reached India by sailing around Africa. In the final analysis, it was a far more practical route than the one sought by Columbus.

⭐

PART
FIVE
*The Vikings,
Belle Starr,
and Lucky
Lindy*

225

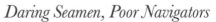
The Vikings have a reputation for being great explorers and skilled sailors. After all, they reached North America 506 years ahead of Columbus. It would be more accurate to describe the Vikings as fearless seamen but rather poor navigators. Others were far more advanced in navigational skills. Still, the primitive methods used by the Vikings to negotiate distant seas proved to be an asset rather than a liability, allowing them to discover more lands by accident than they ever would have by design.

The Norsemen were one-dimensional sailors. They did not use maps or instruments to guide their ships. They navigated by instinct and acquired knowledge—guided by the direction of the winds and the positions of the sun and stars. They tried not to venture too far from land, using their knowledge of seabirds to estimate distance and direction. They were adept at following a steady east-west longitudinal course when the skies were clear. But they were always getting lost in storms that blew them off course and sometimes far beyond their intended destinations.

That is how they found Greenland, and that is what happened to Bjarni Herjolfsson in the year 986 A.D. He was sailing from Iceland to Greenland when his vessel was caught in a vicious storm. When the skies finally cleared, he was off the coast of a strange land, which he realized was far to the west of Greenland.

Without knowing where he was, Bjarni Herjolfsson had blundered upon present-day Newfoundland, off the northeast coast of Canada. Herjolfsson returned to Greenland and told the Norse colonists about a flat land covered with woods he had seen far beyond their colony.

Contrary to common belief, it was Herjolfsson, not Leif Ericsson, who first reached North America. He simply did not go ashore. Some fifteen years passed before Ericsson decided to seek out the new land and determine if it was suitable for colonization. Upon reaching Newfoundland in 1001 (the date is in dispute), Ericsson and his 35-man crew constructed huts and spent the winter there before returning to Greenland. He named the new land Vinland the Good, which may indicate that he might have sailed south along the North American coastline because it is believed that grapevines were not present on Newfoundland.

A third expedition to the new land set out in 1004, led by Ericsson's brother, Thorvald. He and his crew wintered in the huts built by Leif and the following summer explored the coastline of Newfoundland. Some historians believe Thorvald might have crossed the Bay of St. Lawrence and reached the North American mainland. At some point the Norsemen were attacked by natives, and Thorvald was killed. The crew returned his body to Greenland for burial.

The fourth Viking visit to North America was in 1010. Thorfinn Karlsefin, a Greenland trader, accompanied by 250 settlers, established a colony on Newfoundland Island. It survived for three years. Some historians believe Thorfinn or members from his colony sailed along the mainland coast as far south as present-day Long Island. Others have expressed doubt their explorations were that far ranging. Attacks by natives, called "Skrellings" by the Norsemen, forced the colonists to abandon their enterprise and return to Greenland. The remains of Ericsson's huts and Karlsefin's settlement are still in evidence on the coast of Newfoundland today.

The fifth known Viking visit (there might have been others) began in 1356, still 136 years ahead of Columbus. It might have been the most far-reaching of all the pre-Columbian explorations of North America. Ironically, it was not even supposed to take place.

The saga began when a Norwegian sea captain named Paul Knutson was dispatched to Greenland under orders by King Magnus of Norway and Sweden to restore the Christian faith to backsliding Norsemen living on the island. Once he reached Greenland, Knutson heard tales about a great land to the west and decided to go see it for himself, leaving the renewal of the Greenlanders' faith to others.

Knutson and his men sailed away and were not seen again for eight years. It was assumed they had become victims of the sea or perhaps of the natives. But in 1364, a few of Knutson's men re-

That's
Not
in My
American
History
Book

turned to Greenland and reported that most of those on the expedition had died or were lost, including Knutson. Apparently, the party was divided with one group exploring the coastal area while a second probed the shoreline along Hudson Bay. Few details of the venture were ever documented, and the movements of the Norsemen remain a mystery.

The Knutson expedition was not at all typical of Viking explorations. Rarely were they driven by a simple desire for discovery. Commerce and colonization were much stronger motivators. Just like everyone else, the Vikings had to earn a living. For a time they did so by plundering the coastal towns of western Europe. Later, they turned to trade. By the ninth century, they already had established colonies in Iceland and Greenland and set up a thriving trade with the homeland.

The Vikings arrived at Iceland in about 870 A.D. Irish settlers were there ahead of them, but the Norsemen drove them out. Eric the Red (father of Leif Ericsson) discovered Greenland while lost at sea and later colonized the island. It was named Greenland as a public relations ruse to encourage settlers to go there.

The image of Viking longboats crossing stormy, open seas in search of new lands is another myth that deserves clarification. The Vikings actually constructed two types of boats. The longboat was a raiding vessel, capable of carrying a large number of warriors and operating along rugged coastlines. The boat that carried Norsemen to distant lands beyond the North Atlantic was the "knorr." It was a short, one-mast vessel, 40 to 60 feet in length and capable of transporting cargoes. It also was an exceptionally seaworthy craft capable of withstanding the violent storms of the North Atlantic.

The Vikings were noted for being fearless when venturing into strange waters. There was a reason for their bravery. They believed the Earth was shaped like a giant dish with land masses around the rim to hold in the water. This being the case, they reasoned, it would be impossible to sail off of the edge of the world.

There is no doubt they reached North America well ahead of Columbus. The only debate centers on the extent of their explorations. Did their journeys take them to what is now the United States? Did Karlsefin and his men actually reach Long Island?

Norse relics have been unearthed in Canada and the United States. A Viking sword, ax, and the iron handle of a shield were discovered in a grave in what is now Canada's Ontario Province.

Near Newport, Rhode Island, are the remnants of a tower that might have been constructed by Norsemen—perhaps by the Knutson party. And there is the most controversial sign of all—the Kensington Stone. It is a rock with what appear to be Norse runes carved on its surface describing a conflict between Vikings and North American natives. It was discovered in central Minnesota. Its authenticity is a subject of continuing debate.

The Knutson party spent eight years in the New World, enough time to conduct wide-ranging explorations along the American coastline and, possibly, the interior of the continent. Had Knutson survived and returned to Greenland to record his adventures, we would know the answers.

There does remain one mystery that defies solution: Many centuries after the Vikings had gone home, French explorers in the American Midwest encountered a phenomenon that has never been fully explained. They came upon a tribe of native Americans in the upper Missouri Valley. Their skin was unusually light and many had blue-gray eyes. It is a genetic puzzle that still baffles the experts.

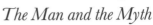

Washington
The Man and the Myth

If we are to believe traditional history, George Washington was the greatest moralist since Christ, the greatest warrior since Alexander the Great, and the wisest ruler since Solomon. Something less than the legend that overshadows him was the man himself.

In reality, George Washington was subject to the same human frailties inherent in all men. Far from the wooden icon portrayed by history, he was a complex personality who could be warm and friendly or aloof and unyieldingly stubborn. Fortunately, those negative traits proved to be an asset in dealing with an equally arrogant Continental Congress; and a less stubborn man might have given up after suffering as many battlefield defeats as Washington experienced in the darkest days of the nation's struggle for independence. Through it all, he was plagued by personal problems—most of them rising from a strained relationship with a domineering, emotionally troubled mother.

Many of the myths attached to Washington flowed from the pen of Mason Locke Weems, author of *The Life of George Washington*. Unfortunately, Weems's flawed biography became a source for subsequent works. His cherry tree story is an example of an innocent tale that became mythical history.

According to the yarn, young Washington decided to try out his new hatchet by felling a cherry tree. When confronted by his father, the future president confessed: "I cannot tell a lie. It was I who chopped down the cherry tree." It was a nice little morality anecdote that fit comfortably into school textbooks, the lesson being that we should all be as forthcoming with the truth as was the father of our country. Regrettably, the story has no basis in fact.

Weems had a proclivity for making up stories to spice up his biographies. Although he never recanted this particular story, he did confess that he made up other parts of the Washington biography as well as parts of his book, *The Life of William Penn*, including a very detailed—and fictitious—description of Penn signing his famous treaty with the Indians. Somewhat ironic is the fact that Weems was a clergyman.

And the *real* George Washington? Physically, he stood six feet tall and weighed a little over 200 pounds. He was big-boned and had large hands. Under a powdered wig was a shock of reddish-brown hair. Blue eyes looked out from beneath drooping lids. His cheeks were pocked, the result of a childhood bout with smallpox. According to legend, he never smiled because he did not want to show his wooden false teeth. If truth be known, he did not smile in those old portraits because he probably was distraught at having to sit still for the artist. In fact, Washington was a social animal who enjoyed the adulation heaped upon him. Indeed, he had false teeth; but they were not wooden. They were carved from ivory by an accomplished dentist named John Greenwood, who implanted several animal teeth in the plates for practical chewing purposes.

Washington was gracious and charming. He enjoyed dancing and flirting with the adoring women who flocked around him at social events. It was rumored that he engaged in extramarital affairs. He loved to play cards, go fox hunting, and fish. He was a social drinker who prefered wine and beer to hard liquor. He had his own whiskey still, a winery, and brewed his own beer. Although he grew tons of tobacco, he did not smoke.

He exuded strength and inspired confidence. He had an ability to remain calm in the most trying circumstances, but also possessed an unpredictable temper that might manifest itself at the most unexpected times—a trait that, no doubt, was effective in keeping his political enemies off guard.

Washington was born on February 11, 1732, not February 22 as noted on modern calendars, because he was born when the Julian calendar was still in use. His parents were Augustus and Mary Ball Washington, and young Washington grew up on a farm near Fredericksburg, Virginia. Although well off, his father was not exceedingly wealthy. Augustus Washington died when George was eleven years old. George's mother, who was self-centered and demanding, would have a contentious relationship with her son until the day she died. Unable to get along with his mother, 16-year-old George went to live with his half-brother, Lawrence. He accompanied Lawrence to Barbados in the West Indies on a business trip and contracted the smallpox that left his face scarred for life.

That's
Not
in My
American
History
Book

When Lawrence died in 1752, he left Mount Vernon and his land holdings to George, then only twenty years old. Contrary to common belief, it was Lawrence, not George, who built Mount Vernon.

Washington joined the Virginia Militia when he was twenty-one. He did so against the wishes of his mother, who wanted him to stay at home and take care of her. At twenty-two, he was placed in command of an army sent deep into the Ohio wilderness to engage the French. In his first major battle, he was defeated and had to surrender Fort Necessity. However, he later distinguished himself in a successful assault on Fort Duquesne in 1758.

With the conclusion of the French and Indian War, Washington returned to Mount Vernon and, at age twenty-nine, married Martha Dandridge Custis, a wealthy widow who could not tolerate his mother's strange behavior. Washington became obsessed with acquiring land and eventually would own 110,000 acres. He raised vast fields of tobacco, worked by slaves, and his stables produced some of the finest racehorses in Virginia.

Washington was not one of the firebrands of the American Revolution. He argued against Colonial separation from Great Britain in the Virginia House of Commons and the Continental Congress until it became apparent that armed conflict was inevitable. His support of the Crown cost him an election in 1775, when he was soundly defeated in a bid for the Virginia House of Burgesses.

When the revolution became a shooting war, Washington accepted command of the Continental Army. He was chosen not for his military expertise, but because of his name. The Congress correctly assumed his popularity and status would help with recruiting. He was a good organizer and leader of men. A good strategist, Washington possessed an ability to see the broad overview; but he was only adequate as a battlefield commander. In his first major engagement against the British, he almost lost his entire 10,500-man army on Long Island. He was saved by a rainstorm that left a heavy fog cloaking the island, allowing him to evacuate 9,000 men. Gen. William Howe might have captured Washington's entire force and ended the rebellion by landing troops from nearby ships but, inexplicably, failed to do so.

In the early stages of the war, General Howe and his crack British troops outmaneuvered and defeated Washington's poorly trained Continentals in almost every engagement, leaving one quarter of his 16,000-man army dead, wounded, or captured. In the bittercold winter of 1778, Washington lost 2,000 troops to desertion, many of whom went to Philadelphia to join the British Army. On several occasions, the Congress came close to firing him.

In the darkest days of the revolution, Washington held his small army together by the sheer force of his will. However, his most important decision of the war might have been to hire a German military expert named Friedrich von Steuben to train his troops and assist him with battlefield strategy.

Most of Washington's victories resulted from carefully selected engagements in which he had superior forces in the field. They were battles fought to boost the morale of his troops and that of the Continental Congress, rather than for strategic gain.

In October of 1781, at the head of an army of 15,000 (including 8,000 French troops), Washington finally trapped 7,500 redcoats under General Cornwallis at Yorktown, ending the war. He had lost almost every major battle in which he participated—but he won the war.

Washington was always pragmatic when it came to business matters, a trait that became apparent following the war. Upon accepting the job of commander in chief, he graciously offered to

Father of Our Country George Washington holds such a lofty position in American history that he is obscured by myths about him. *National Archives & Records Administration*

That's
Not
in My
American
History
Book

234

forgo a $500-per-month salary and work for expenses. With the end of the war he turned in some $400,000 worth of expenses. (Later, when he became president, Washington offered to forgo his $25,000-per-year salary and work for expenses, prompting the Congress to say thanks, but no thanks, George.)

Although Washington eventually was paid, many of his officers and men were not. In 1883, the unpaid troops staged a rebellion at Newburgh, New York, threatening to take over the government. Addressing them, Washington demonstrated a flair for theatrics. Using a pair of spectacles for his prop, he told the troops: "I have not only grown gray but also blind in the service of my country," gaining immediate support from the men. He then read a communication promising that all wages would be paid—which, if not technically a lie, certainly was not the truth. Most of the men were never paid.

Seldom acknowledged by historians is Washington's troubled personal life. He and his mother were estranged for most of his adult life. She did not attend his wedding and never visited his home, probably at the insistence of his wife, Martha. There are indications his mother suffered bouts of mental illness. Although she was wealthy, she would wear the same dress day after day for months on end, until the garment was virtually in tatters. In spite of her wealth, she constantly harrassed her son for money. On one occasion, she even wrote a letter to the Virginia assembly complaining that George would not give her enough money to live on, and accusing him of neglecting her. Mary Washington never expressed pride in the accomplishments of her famous son.

Washington was sixty-seven when he contracted a throat virus. He died not from the virus but at the hands of his doctors, who drained half of the blood from his body in less than twelve hours. At the end, he pleaded with his doctors to, "Let me go off quickly, I cannot last long."

What would last was the legend that cloaked the man who became known as "The Father of Our Country."

Bibliography

Books

Abernathy, Thomas P. *The Burr Conspiracy.* Oxford: Oxford Press, 1954.

Adams, John T. *The Adams Family.* Boston: Little Brown, 1930.

Athearn, Robert G. *The American Heritage New Illustrated History of the United States,* 16 vols. New York: Dell, 1963.

Beebe, Lucius, and Charles Clegg. *The American West: The Pictorial Epic of a Continent.* New York: E.P. Dutton, 1955.

Boyer, Paul S. *The Enduring Vision: A History of the American People.* Lexington, MA: D.C. Heath, 1990.

Burns, Ric and Ken. *The Civil War: An Illustrated History.* New York: Alfred A. Knopf, 1994.

Capps, Benjamin. *The Old West: The Great Chiefs.* Alexandria, VA: Time-Life Books, 1997.

Carey, John, ed. *Eyewitness to History.* New York: Avon, 1990.

Chaplin, J. P. *Rumor, Fear and the Madness of Crowds.* New York: Ballantine, Bantam, 1975.

Clark,, Champ. *The Civil War. The Assassination: Death of the President.* New York: Time-Life, 1987.

Davis, Kenneth C. *Don't Know Much About History.* New York: William Morrow, 1994.

Davis, Mac. *Sports Shorts* New York: Bantam, 1963.

Dees, A. J. *Southern Farm and Land Almanac.* Middlebrook, AL, 1943.

De Tocqueville, Alexis. *Democracy in America.* 1835 Reprint, New York: Vintage Books, 1954.

Falls, Cyril. *Great Military Battles.* London: Spring Books, 1964.

Freidel, Frank. *The Presidents of the United States.* Washington, D.C.: National Geographic, 1964.

Gantry, John A. *The American Nation: A History of the United States.* New York: Harper & Row, 1979.

Grum, Bernard. *The Timetables of History.* 3d ed. New York: Simon & Schuster, 1991.

Guinness Book of World Records. American ed. New York: Bantam, 1998.

Horan, James D. *Authentic Wild West Series: The Lawmen, Accounts by Eyewitnesses and the Lawmen Themselves.* New York: Gramercy, 1996.

Howard, Rex. *Texas Guidebook,* 4th Edition. Grand Prairie, TX: Lo Ray, 1962.

Howard, Ted. *Voices of the American Revolution.* New York: Bantam, 1975.

How in the World? Pleasantville, NY: Reader's Digest, 1990.

Hunt, Gaillard. *Life in America One Hundred Years Ago.* New York: Harper & Brothers, 1914.

Irving, Wallace, and others. *The Book of Lists.* New York: Bantam, 1977

Irving, Wallace and others. *The Book of Lists 2.* New York: Bantam, 1962.

Janda, Kenneth. *The Challenge of Democracy.* Boston: Houghton Mifflin, 1987.

Jarolimek, John and Bertha Davis. *Lands of Promise: Western Hemisphere Setting and Settlement.* New York: MacMillan, 1974.

Josephy, Alvin M. Jr. *500 Nations: An Illustrated History of North American Indians.* New York: Alfred A. Knopf, 1994.

Klapthor, Margaret. *The First Ladies.* Washington, D.C.: White House

That's
Not
in My
American
History
Book

236

Historical Association, National Geographic, 1989.

Kuttner, Paul. *History's Trickiest Questions*. New York: Henry Holt and Company, 1992.

Labaree, Benjamin. The *Boston Tea Party*. Oxford Press, 1964.

Leavitt, Jerome. *By Land, By Sea, By Air, The Story of American Transportation*. New York: Putnam's, 1969.

Lincoln: An Illustrated Biography. New York: Alfred Knopf, 1992.

Loewen, James W. *Lies My Teacher Told Me: Everything Your American History Textbook Got Wrong*. New York: New Press, 1995.

Long, E. John. *America's National Capital*. Garden City, NY: Doubleday, 1959.

Morgan, Kay Summersby. *Past Forgetting: My Love Affair with Dwight D. Eisenhower*. New York: Simon and Schuster, 1976.

The New York Public Library American History Desk Reference. New York: MacMillan, 1997.

Nye, Edgar Wilson. *Bill Nye's Comic History of the United States*. Chicago: Thompson & Thomas, 1906.

O'Dwyer, William. *History by Contract: The Beginning of Motorized Aviation*. Leutershausen, W. Germany: Fritz Majer & Sohm, 1978.

Ramsell, C. W. *Texas in Reconstruction*. San Antonio, TX: Naylor, n.d.

Randolph, Stella. *Lost Flights of Gustave Whitehead*. Washington, D.C.: Places, Inc., 1937.

Ray, G. B.. *Murder at the Corners*. San Antonio, TX: Naylor, 1957.

Richardson, Rupert N. *Texas, The Lone Star State*. San Antonio, TX: Naylor, 1951.

Robinson, Nugent. *History of the World. Vol. II, Mighty and Decisive Battles*. New York: P. F. Collier, 1887.

Savage, William W. *Cowboy Life: Reconstructing an American Myth*. Norman: University of Oklahoma Press, 1975.

A Sense of History: The Best Writings from the Pages of American Heritage. Boston: Houghton Mifflin, 1985.

Storer, Doug. *The Most Amazing But True*. New York: Fawcett, 1960.

Strange Stories, Amazing Facts. Pleasantville, NY: Reader's Digest, 1978.

Syrett, Harold C. *Andrew Jackson: His Contribution to the American Tradition*. Indianapolis: Bobbs-Merrill, 1953.

Virga, Vincent. *Eyes of the Nation: A Visual History of the United States*. New York: Alfred A. Knopf, 1997.

Virginia: History, Government, Geography. New York: Scribner's, 1957.

Washburn, Wilcomb. *The Indian and the White Man*. New York: New York University Press, 1964.

We the People: The Story of the United States Capital. Washington, D.C.: National Geographic Society, 1988.

Wirth, Fremont P. *The Development of America*. Boston: American Book Co., 1937.

Booklets

Gibson, Jon L. *Poverty Point*. Baton Rouge: Louisiana Division of Archaeology, 1996.

Green, Richard L. *A Salute to Black Pioneers*. Chicago: Empak, 1986.

Newman, Robert W., and Nancy Hawkins. *Louisiana Prehistory*. Baton Rouge: Museum of Natural Science, 1993.

Magazines

Archaeology Magazine
Dallas Times Herald Magazine
Family Circle
Newsweek
National Enquirer
NRTA Journal
Popular Mechanics
Southern Living
Texas Monthly Magazine
Time Magazine
USA Weekend
U.S. News and World Report

News Services

Associated Press, New York
National Features Syndicate, Chicago
Tribune Media Services, Chicago
United Press International, New York

Index

★

That's

Not

in My

American

History

Book

That's
Not
in My
American
History
Book

240